ANABAPTIST-MENNONITES

NATIONWIDE USA

Includes Amish and Brethren in Christ

compiled by

C. Nelson Hostetter

Anabaptist-Mennonites
Nationwide USA

Printed in the United States of America.

Library of Congress Number: 97-73969

International Standard Book Number: 1-883294-56-8

Published by
Masthof Press
R.R. 1, Box 20, Mill Road
Morgantown, PA 19543-9701

Contents

Where We Are [*State Statistics and Summaries From Largest To Smallest*] . . 32

Preface

The quiltwork of Anabaptist-related groups in the United States is perplexing to outsiders and insiders alike. Strangers to Anabaptist life are baffled by the many groups and their endless differences and practices. Insiders know something of the story of their own tribe and perhaps a bit about a few nearby and related groups, but even insiders are not always sure where their patch fits on the overall quilt. Indeed, for many insiders and outsiders the patches of Anabaptist life are simply a random assortment of patches.

In this volume, C. Nelson Hostetter has stitched the diverse patches together into a colorful forty-six-patch quilt. It's no wonder that confusion abounds with some forty-six different groups sleeping together under the Anabaptist quilt! Hostetter's tedious quilting will enable insiders to better understand where their own patch fits in the large fabric of Anabaptist life. Strangers to the world of Anabaptism will find a helpful introductory overview to the diversity, color, and size of this unique religious quilt.

A brief overview of each group provides an introduction to their history and distinctive practices. The numerical profile combined with the socio-historical description offers a quick and helpful introduction to each of the forty-six groups.

Hostetter's profile of Anabaptist-related groups in the United States is important for several reasons. At one glance it provides us with a succinct overview of the size and location of Anabaptist communities. His tabulations separate the major bodies from the smaller ones—eleven of the affiliations have more than 100 congregations each; twenty of the subgroups have fewer than ten congregations. The Old Order Amish have the most congregations with 1,055. The two largest Mennonite bodies (Mennonite Church and General Conference), now in the process of integration, have a total of 953 congregations. In addition to the national view,

Hostetter provides a state-by-state breakdown which shows the concentration and diversity of subgroups within each state.

Finally, this is much more than a statistical tabulation that offers a directory of groups and numbers. This volume offers a handy and convenient introduction to Anabaptist life in the United States. We are indebted to C. Nelson Hostetter for stitching our story together in a new way that will help us better understand who we are, where we come from, and where we are today.

Donald B. Kraybill, Ph.D.
Provost, Messiah College
Grantham, Pennsylvania

Introduction

For several years my friends and peers have encouraged me to write this book. As a young person I became intrigued by my religious roots that can be traced through Brethren in Christ, Lutheran, Mennonite, Old Order River Brethren, and United Zion lines.

The twenty-four years that I served both as a volunteer and supported staff person for an inter-Mennonite program and the seven years in a similar capacity for several inter-church organizations have intensified my research and study efforts.

It started as an effort to make sure all congregations, districts, and fellowships of the Anabaptist-Mennonites were connected into the network of Mennonite Disaster Service. It continued as a statistics hobby for several years and then developed into this more serious book project.

I wish to take this opportunity to thank those who have assisted me in a special way: to my good wife Esther for her editing, secretarial, and typing support, and being loving and patient as I learned to use the computer; to the directory staffs of the larger Anabaptist-Mennonite groups; to the Brethren in Christ bishops' offices; for access to conference reports and committee meeting minutes of some groups; for the candid and open dialogue I was privileged to share with certain leadership persons by correspondence, telephone conversations, and visits in my rather extensive travel. And my deep appreciation goes to the management and staff of Masthof Press who serves as the publisher.

Some individuals who have helped me in direct ways are Aden Gingerich of Farmington, New Mexico; Rich Preheim and Wesley Prieb of Newton and Hillsboro, Kansas; Aden Yoder of

Goshen, Indiana, and Sarasota, Florida; Henry and Leroy Beachy and Ben Raber of Holmes County, Ohio; David Luthy of Aylmer, Ontario; and Amos Hoover, Donald Kraybill, and Stephen Scott of Lancaster County, Pennsylvania. To those I might have missed who should have been included in this listing, please forgive the oversight.

I offer this to you, the reader, in partnership as we work together toward the goal Jesus set for us in His Highpriestly prayer as recorded in John 7:11:

"That they may be one."

C. Nelson Hostetter
Akron, Pennsylvania

Anabaptist-Mennonite Beginnings

In the year 1525 about fifteen young adults, most in their thirties, were meeting for serious Bible study and earnest prayer in a home in Zurich, Switzerland. During those sessions together they felt a conviction to rebaptize each other, and the new Anabaptist way of Christian life was established.

Infant baptism, demanded by the state church, was now history for this small group. Since then this third way of response to the Gospel has been followed by many until today there are a million-plus practicing Anabaptists around the world.

Anabaptism can be detailed in four basic terms: Adult baptism, baptized again, believers' baptism, or re-baptism. I remember well, during my days of travel for a church program, often in the Deep South, I would need to repeat carefully the word **Ana**baptist, because I was misunderstood to have said **anti**-Baptist.

For about a decade, prior to 1525, several individual reformers broke from and spoke out against the state stranglehold on the religious life of that era. The issue of separation of church and state was the second major concern of the new Anabaptists. Two other very important considerations were a personal faith in Christ and repentance for past sins.

During the next decade a Catholic priest, in the north of Holland, was observing and carefully following the development and expansion of the new Anabaptist wave. Menno Simons struggled for a period of time between the practices of the state church and the teachings of the Scriptures as he was beginning to understand them. Finally in 1536, Menno declared his personal faith and joined the Anabaptists, whose network was growing in spite of intense persecution to the members and martyrdom for the leadership persons.

Menno was born in 1496, so he was a mature forty years of age when he made the change from Catholic priest to Anabaptist leader. He married and fathered several children. He was forced to live in seclusion, and on occasion moved underground in his leadership role. The reality that "even his wife and children lived in danger" was difficult for him. He died a natural death in 1561. His main contribution to the new movement was his clear and concise writings which were a Christ-like model for those times, and are a certainty and help in contemporary life.

From his studies of the Scriptures, Menno called for added convictions to those of other Anabaptist leaders. He began to write and teach about Holy community; mutual aid; sharing of resources; support to widows, their children, and the poor; sister/brotherhood among believers; simple life-style; nonresistance; nonviolence; peacemaking; and the servanthood stance. All are imperative in the total life of both the changed individual and the committed congregation.

The new dimensions of Christian life listed above are today observed to a greater or lesser degree by the broad spectrum of present-day Anabaptist-Mennonites. But perhaps their greatest bond now can be taken from Menno Simons' wider statement based on Matthew 25, verses 34 to 40: "True evangelical faith cannot lie dormant. It clothes the naked. It feeds the hungry. It comforts the sorrowful. It shelters the destitute. It serves those that harm it. It binds up that which is wounded. It has become all things to all people." Today you will find this quotation on plaques in many homes, on the bulletin boards and walls of classrooms in many churches, and often in the denominational communications and media.

The denominational name "Mennonite" was first used as a nickname, but through the centuries it has become an accepted label in the milieu of Christendom. The Anabaptists who have been faithful from the Reformation period, now living in community, congregations, clusters, colonies, districts, fellowships, and settlements across the United States, fall into three mainstreams: the Swiss Brethren, the Hutterites, and the Mennonites. The Church of the Brethren, with headquarters in Elgin, Illinois, is currently the largest of the Swiss Brethren. The Hutterites, founded by Jakob Hutter who was martyred in 1537, are located in their colonies across the northern prairie states. The Mennonites, with others from the Menno Simons line, have spread nationwide except into Nevada, New Hampshire, Rhode Island, and Utah.

More than 4,000 Anabaptists lost their lives in the first one hundred years, most by fire and water—at the stake or by drowning—at the hands of both Catholics and Protestants. Some were beheaded. Such trials and tribulation brought an amazing growth in those early times.

Anabaptist-Mennonites, now with a million members world wide, have formed numerous disaster and relief committees which operate programs to help their own and assist others suffering from famine, natural disasters, and wars. The first somewhat organized relief effort was by Dutch Mennonites to aid their own people fleeing persecution in Switzerland, and also to help refugees in eastern France to find new homes in the States at the invitation of Quaker leader William Penn.

In the 1870s there were programs to bring many hurting fellow-Mennonites from Europe to Canada and the United States. And again after World War I, and during and after World War II, many suffering Mennonite refugees from Russia and Eastern Europe were helped to immigrate to both North and South America, enlarging established communities and starting new settlements. A conservative estimate of at least $60 million in value was shared last year, around the globe. The Mennonite Central Committee, formed in 1920, a partnership of Canadian and United States Mennonites, Brethren in Christ, and Amish, provides leadership for these expressions of compassion, faith, hope, and love.

Anabaptist-Mennonite Groups

	Congregations Districts Fellowships	Baptized Membership
1. Mennonite Church Conferences Congregations (MC)	811	83,310
2. Old Order Amish Districts (OOA)	1,055	60,885
3. General Conference Mennonite Congregations (GC)	142	25,941
4. Mennonite Brethren (MB)	157	22,432
5. Brethren in Christ Churches (BiC)	188	18,548
6. Old Order Mennonites (OOM)	124	13,847
7. Groffdale Conference (OOMGC)	43	5,896
8. Weaverland Conference (OOMWC)	31	4,849
9. Stauffer Group (OOMSG)	7	702
10. Wisler Conference (OOMWIC)	6	673
11. Unaffiliated (OOMU)	14	460
12. Ohio Wisler Group (OOMOWG)	4	356
13. Reidenbach Old Order Mennonites (ROOM)	10	338
14. Wenger/Weaver Group (OOMWWG)	3	318
15. Noah Hoover Group (OOMNHG)	4	211
16. John Martin Group (OOMJMG)	2	44
17. Dual Conference (GC/MC) Congregations (DC)	151	11,725
18. Church of God in Christ, Mennonite (CGCM)	107	11,289
19. Mennonite Church Independent Conferences (MCIC)	168	10,465
20. Conservative Mennonite Conference (CM)	100	9,875
21. Beachy Amish Mennonite (BAM)	102	7,406
22. Mennonite Church, Unaffiliated, Congregations (MCU)	110	5,470
23. Evangelical Mennonite Church (EMC)	28	4,266
24. New Order Amish (NOA)	44	2,488
25. Mennonite Church Independent Districts (MCID)	18	2,396

26. Independent Mennonite Congregations (IM)	12	2,254
27. Mennonite Fellowship Churches (MFC)	41	1,861
28. Amish Mennonite (AM)	12	1,256
29. Mennonite Christian Fellowship (MCF)	19	1,056
30. Anabaptist Christian Fellowship (ACF)	19	973
31. Conservative Mennonite, Unaffiliated (CMU)	13	899
32. United Zion Churches (UZC)	13	856
33. Mennonite/Church of the Brethren (M/CoB)	9	691
34. Evangelical Mennonite Brethren (EMB)	4	501
35. Old Colony Mennonite (OCM)	1	339
36. Amish Mennonite, Unaffiliated (AMU)	8	318
37. Old Order River Brethren Churches (OORB)	5	317
38. Reformed Mennonite (RM)	9	275
39. Mennonite Evangelical Churches (MEC)	3	208
40. Reinlander Mennonite Church (RMC)	1	170
41. Mennonite Church/Other Denominations (MCOD)	3	163
42. Evangelical Mennonite Mission Conference (EMMC)	1	154
43. Kleine Gemeinde Community (KG)	1	65
44. Tri-Conference: GC/MB/MC (TriC)	1	60
45. Mennonite Brethren/Mennonite Church (MB/MC)	1	35
46. United Mennonite (UM)	1	12

Menno Cousins
Across the United States

The Anabaptist-Mennonites, because of their suffering from various acts of persecution in Europe, were among the early emigrants from the old world to the new one across the seas. The first group to arrive in 1683 were from Dutch roots, coming through Germany. Then, in those turn-of-the-century decades, others followed. There were many family units, some singles, and married men who left wives and children behind with promises to return for them. All were willing to risk hardship of ocean travel and the uncertainty of a new and almost unknown world. It was another step of faith along the way for them to move toward religious freedom and the privilege to worship, live, and serve according to their collective and individual conscience.

These pilgrim pioneers landed in Philadelphia and set up their first settlements about twenty miles north in Bucks and Montgomery Counties, and seventy miles west in and around Lancaster. They enjoyed the freedom of their new home and quickly set to clearing land; building simple houses and barns; planting, growing, and harvesting crops; and putting together strong Christian communities. My ancestor, Jacob Hostetter, arrived from Switzerland in 1712 and settled on the south side of Lancaster City, in the county where I and other eighth-generation descendants now reside.

In the recent two centuries, from about 1800 to almost the year 2000, the Anabaptist-Mennonites have gone through both exciting and disappointing cycles. There has been growth with membership now numbering over 302,000 in 3,474 congregational units. Churches and fellowships have been planted and new settlements have been established. However, in some places congregations have closed and communities have become extinct.

The main focus of the next section is to list and provide statistical information for the forty-five or so subgroups that are now organized and meeting for worship, fellowship, nurture, ministry, and service in "the Third Way" and living together as contemporary Menno Cousins.

Who We Are

Mennonite Church
Conferences Congregations

This is the largest of the subgroups, now stretching from New England to Florida and the territory of Puerto Rico, and westward across the central and southern states, the vast Midwest from Texas to Montana and North Dakota, and across the Rocky Mountains to the Pacific Coast with new congregations now in Alaska and Hawaii.

In the mid-1800s loosely organized conferences were formed from Mennonite and Amish-Mennonite congregations and clusters in the central states and eastern Pennsylvania. The first more structured organization was established as the Old Mennonite Church in 1898. An official name change to the Mennonite Church was approved in 1971. Today this group meets nationwide in biannual sessions. The district conferences meet on an annual basis while the largest, Lancaster, meets on a semi-annual schedule.

John F. Funk, 1835-1930, and John S. Coffman, 1848-1899, were the two leaders who emerged during the last half of the nineteenth century to bring about some changes to a more active denomination. They, along with some local Mennonite leaders, were influenced by their counterparts in the mainline denominations of that day, while others, at the local level, were rigid in their stand on Mennonite separation and withdrawal, most certainly from the wider denominational scene. Funk and Coffman introduced Sunday Schools, revival meetings, and a periodical, the *Herald of Truth,* oriented to faith foundations based on biblical study and understanding, with a German companion which helped move from the emphasis on language. The organizational process was also Coffman and Funk's contribution to that time of transition. In the first half of this century, two leaders who inspired this group were Daniel Kauffman (1865-1944) and Harold S. Bender (1895-1962). Bender's *Anabaptist Vision*, written in 1944 as a paper for presentation to a national ecumenical meeting, has influenced many to remain true to the faith of the founding fathers in this last half of the twentieth century.

Important tenets of the faith for this largest group today are the Lordship of Christ, faithful discipleship, peacemaking, congregational support to the family unit, and the priesthood of each member. The group now sponsors and operates two seminaries, three colleges, at least fourteen parochial secondary schools, and about thirty-five elementary schools. They also maintain a publishing house at Scottdale, Pennsylvania, with a weekly denominational periodical, the *Gospel Herald*.

There are seventeen organized conferences, most along geographic lines, with over 800 congregations and a membership of 83,300. About one-third of these are found within Pennsylvania. Mennonite Church Conference congregations average about 100 members each. This reflects in one way the earlier distance limits with horse and buggy prior to the arrival of the automobile. Another consideration is the continued concern that the smaller congregation provides a better opportunity for closer community.

This is a listing of the conferences, nationwide, today: Allegheny, Atlantic Coast, Franconia, Franklin, Gulf States, Illinois, Indiana-Michigan, Iowa-Nebraska, Lancaster, New York, North Central, Ohio, Puerto Rico, Rocky Mountain, South Central, Southeast, and Virginia. The Lancaster Conference is the largest with 19,800 members, and the smallest is the North Central with a membership of 520. Mennonite Church congregations are found in thirty-nine states, the District of Columbia, and Puerto Rico. Headquarters and staff are located at Elkhart, Indiana.

General Conference
Mennonite Congregations

The General Conference Mennonites, third largest group in the States, were organized in southeast Iowa in 1860, bringing together representatives and congregations from eastern Ohio,

Pennsylvania, Illinois, and Canada. In those days they set themselves aside from the larger Mennonite and Amish-Mennonite groups by their first constitution which included these most important beliefs: decisions should be made by the congregation, less emphasis upon external forms, greater freedom of the Holy Spirit in their circles, and questioning the use of the lot in calling out leadership. John H. Oberholtzer, an ordained minister from the Skippack area of eastern Pennsylvania, was selected as their leader. One of the hopes of the new General Conference leadership, in their early pilgrimage, was to assist all Mennonites to unite.

In the decades from the 1870s into the '90s, at least 12,000 Russian Mennonites resettled in Minnesota, South Dakota, Nebraska, and Kansas. They seemed to find greater fellowship with the scattered newly organized group rather than with the larger groups where they found more local community life with Dutch influence, whereas the Swiss were more open to expansion with the recent arrivals. Later, during and after World War I, those emigrating from Europe to the States found sister/brotherhood with the General Conference communities, again increasing congregations and membership.

From the 1920s to the mid-'30s, there were transfers of leadership persons, ministers, college professors, and influential lay persons from the Mennonite Church to the General Conference. With the addition of their families this totaled several hundred more members. This move was concentrated in northern Indiana and northwest Ohio, but there were also similar transfers in the east and the far west. Another independent group, the Central Conference Mennonites with Amish roots, joined the Central District of the General Conference in 1946, bringing more than 3,000 members.

Today there are 142 congregations with over 25,900 members in the GC family. Approximately one-third are located across the state of Kansas where Newton, just north of Wichita, is national headquarters. The GCs are located in fifteen states and organized into four geographical districts: Central, Eastern, Northern, and Western. Seventy percent of the GCs west of the Mississippi River are of Russian Mennonite lineage. Both United States and Canadian districts meet together in triennial sessions. They are associated with the MCs in a seminary at Elkhart, Indiana, and operate colleges in Kansas and Ohio. They maintain a printing house in North Newton, Kansas, and publish a periodical, *The Mennonite*, twice monthly.

An important conviction of the early Anabaptists which the GCs practice today is that decision making and discipline should be exercised by each congregation.

Dual Conference (GC/MC) Congregations

The first Dual Conference congregations were planted early in 1962. Those were the Kansas City, Kansas, and Columbus, Ohio, Rainbow and Neil Avenue churches. They are now established congregations, each with staff meeting the needs of their members and surrounding neighborhoods. They are the products of the combined outreach efforts of the South Central MC Conference with Western GC District and the Central GC District with the Ohio MC Conference.

During the next decade congregations and smaller fellowships were formed on the DC pattern in suburban areas and near several university complexes. A number of congregations grew out of a relatively small nucleus from each conference group living within a certain area.

The Oak Grove congregation near Smithville, Ohio, with about 450 members, was the first larger and rural church to apply for DC affiliation early in the '70s. The main issue again was congregational versus conference decision making and leadership oversight. Since then other rural congregations have moved in this direction.

In 1994 the GC Districts, the MC Conferences, and their congregations on the Pacific Coast, California, Oregon and Washington State along with Idaho and Arizona, merged. All of these congregations cooperate in combined ministries. Illinois, Kansas, and Texas each have a number of DC congregations. It is possible that the next block of churches to merge will be in Colorado, New Mexico, and the Texas Panhandle. This has already happened in some locations in those states. There are now 150 congregations and fellowships, with about 11,700 members in thirty states in the Dual Conference faith family. Also, there are about eighty-five congregations in Canada, including Ontario and the eastern provinces and some in Alberta, that have been meeting and ministering on a DC basis in recent years. To date the DCs have not started any institutions or programs of their own, but relate to and support through their respective conferences and districts all national, binational, and international ministries. The DCs arrange a get-acquainted fellowship luncheon or dinner at all major meetings of the primary groups.

The first serious discussion regarding possible merger was begun in a joint convention at Bethlehem, Pennsylvania, in the summer of 1983. In August of 1995 the General Conference Mennonites and the Mennonite Church Conferences met in joint sessions at Wichita, Kansas, and voted, by high percentages, to merge within a time frame of several years. Various committees, along with staffs of the counterpart departments, have been and are working on plans for a smooth transition.

For years the two groups have been cooperating in various ministries: joint hymnals and worship books; devotional, nurture, and study materials; relief and service programs and projects; and mutual aid. Presently they are doing overseas mission work together in Bolivia, Hong Kong, and several smaller African countries.

Mennonite Church
Independent Conferences

The Mennonite Independent Conferences and the congregations that relate to them are extensions of the main body, although a few were never a part of the major group. Most made the change due to differences of conviction on both doctrinal and theological standards: a plain dress code; parochial schools; degrees of education; privilege to vote and participate in government at local, state, and national levels; and certain other practices which are detailed in later sections.

The Independent Conference movement spread in the decades after World War II. The larger groups adapted to both modernity and societal changes, due in part to many men returning from their Civilian Public Service (CPS) and I-W terms of alternative service who did not want to impose separated life-styles upon their wives and children. These changes widened the gap between liberal and conservative views. These men and others developed the conviction that the "inner life" was the real test for Christ-like living. Lordship and discipleship took on new meanings. Another trend that brought about the smaller conference movement was the addition of staff by both the national body and the area conferences, and decision-making and discipline by consensus at the congregational base, thus moving authority away from the bishops.

Probably the most important comprehensive concern of this group would be consolidated into a statement drafted at a joint meeting in North Lima, Ohio. "We hereby register our intention to stand fast, by God's grace, on His eternal Word, following the early church in their example of evangelism, instruction, and discipline, walking in God's standard of holiness, regardless of the culture in which we live" (based on Titus 2:11-24).

Today, there are seventeen Independent Conferences of the Mennonite Church. The oldest continuous conference is the Washington Conference, formed back in 1790, now clustered around Hagerstown, Maryland with an outreach into Appalachia, Kentucky. The largest is Eastern Pennsylvania, which separated from the Lancaster Conference in 1968, currently with forty-five congregations. The smallest is the Bible Mennonite Fellowship with three congregations; two in Oregon and one in Montana. There are now a total of 168 congregations with about 10,500 members in twenty-six states and Puerto Rico in Independent Conferences.

Mennonite Church, Unaffiliated Congregations

This group now numbers 110 congregations in twenty-nine states and Washington, D.C., with 5,500 members. You will note that the average membership per congregation is barely fifty members. The largest congregation is the Fairview Mennonite Church at Albany, Oregon, with 350 members.

A majority of these congregations have severed their ties from the Mennonite Church or its area conferences. Rationale for their independence is mainly explained in a different viewpoint of certain scriptures which define the degrees of separated life-style. Related concerns are: women in ministry and family/sexuality issues. On occasion some strong leadership persons fear the loss of power when affiliated with a larger network.

Independent Mennonite Congregations

There are twelve congregations in this group with 2,250 members, located in five states. Most of these had formerly been a part of the General Conference or one of its districts. A few came out of other streams but all have retained the Mennonite label. This group has been influenced by fundamentalism.

All of the congregations are quite active in supporting foreign missionaries who are seconded to inter- or nondenominational mission agencies. Most support a Bible college and Christian radio ministry in Omaha and Lincoln, Nebraska.

Mennonite Church Independent Districts

The Hopewell District in Chester and Lancaster Counties, Pennsylvania, and the Cornerstone Churches in Shenandoah Valley, Virginia, have formed in recent years. They promote cell church and small group concepts and relate to the Atlantic Coast and Virginia Mennonite Conferences for certain support services. Also, they maintain their own headquarters with staffs and mutual aid sharing program, church planting, and overseas mission outreach. Cornerstone sponsors its own Bible college. There are now eighteen congregations with about 2,400 members involved in their direct ministries.

Old Order Amish Districts

The Amish is the second largest group of Anabaptists coming out of the Menno Simons line, now settled across the States. Jacob Ammann, a Swiss Anabaptist leader, believed that the church leaders, especially in eastern France and Switzerland, were not holding to strict separation from the world and that spiritual renewal was needed. Also, the ban, or shunning, was not being practiced by communicants as Ammann believed it should be. He was convicted that the ban should mean a more restricted social relationship with a member who was being disciplined and that, without repentance, excommunication should be practiced. In the decade following 1693 there was much dialogue, and some changes in leadership resulted.

Ammann enforced more separatist ways upon his followers, such as untrimmed beards and hooks and eyes in place of buttons on outer garments of the men. "Social Avoidance" became a major issue, and the question of salvation by grace through faith was the leading theological discussion. The practice of foot washing along with communion was very important.

Early followers of Ammann suffered extreme persecution in some localities of Europe, even more severe than the Mennonites, and today none are found there. They were called "Ammannish" Mennonites, but when the first members arrived in the States, they were called Amish by the English. The most important books they brought with them were the Bible in German, the *Martyrs' Mirror*, and the *Ausbund*, which is still their hymn book, written by a band of Amish who were detained in prison for nearly five years.

The first Amish to arrive in the States settled in Berks County, Pennsylvania, and near Morgantown on the Berks/Lancaster County line in 1736. Later in that century some families moved west while others came directly from Europe to Juniata and Somerset Counties. By the middle of the next century they had settlements in Virginia and the central States. The Amish families moved frequently to new settlements, some almost every decade, searching for more stable and committed communities and better land. Someone has said, "The Amish and the Mennonites always find good dirt." Migration continues today and includes the Old Order and Conservative Mennonites as suburbia, industrial sprawl, and commercial development invade their domain. The concept of faith and living close to the soil is still a very important way of life for them and their children.

Horse and buggy is their basic transportation and horse-drawn implements in their fields for farming clearly identify them. Men, women, and children follow plain and distinctive dress patterns. They have no electricity in their homes; however, they are very ingenious with alternative systems for light and power.

Their worship services are held in homes, barns, or other structures on alternate Sundays with a simple meal together. On "off-Sundays" they visit family and worship in neighboring districts. Each district has a bishop, two ministers, a deacon, and a member of their parochial school board. The students go through the eighth grade, but no higher education is pursued.

The Amish, and certain other ultra-conservative Mennonite groups, do not participate in the Social Security System. Among their larger-than-average families, and with district support, they provide total care for their aged and sickly. The same conviction carries over so that commercial insurance programs are discouraged and a sister/brotherhood sharing fund helps in large losses.

Today the Amish are found in twenty-one states, numbering about 60,800 with over a thousand districts averaging fifty to seventy baptized members each. The concentrations of their people are now in eastern Ohio, southeastern Pennsylvania, and northern Indiana. In recent years they have expanded communities and started new settlements in Kentucky, Michigan, Missouri, and Wisconsin.

Mennonite Brethren

The Mennonite Brethren have retained the greatest influence of Eastern Europe having been born in South Russia in 1860. The first immigrants came to Kansas, Minnesota, Nebraska, and South Dakota between 1874 and 1880. Their first conference was held in Henderson, Nebraska, in 1879.

The early members were often recognized by their bulging coat pockets which carried a well-worn Bible. To them the Christian life begins with a radical inward renewal based on a personal faith in Christ as Savior and Lord. They practice baptism by immersion, following the example of Jesus. Ministers and lay members share boldness and liberty in daily witnessing.

The Krimmer Mennonites, from Crimea in the old country, joined the Mennonite Brethren family in the 1960s. Recent additions have been congregations of Slavic/Ukranian and Korean backgrounds.

National departmental headquarters are located in Fresno, California, and Hillsboro, Kansas. Colleges are also there, with a graduate school and seminary in Fresno.

Today there are 157 congregations with over 22,400 members in nineteen states. A large majority are settled west of the Mississippi River, with a concentration in central California.

Brethren in Christ, Old Order River Brethren, and United Zion Churches

The Brethren in Christ, as now known, have an interesting history. Jacob Engel, now spelled Engle, was the only surviving infant in a group of immigrants making the perilous ninety-day voyage to the new country. All other infants died and were buried at sea. Jacob grew up in a Mennonite family and was converted and joined the church at age eighteen. But he was concerned about the salvation of his soul and dissatisfied with the pouring form of baptism. Engle found several other seekers who also had reservations about their baptism experience. Finally, in 1783, they baptized each other in the Susquehanna River in northern Lancaster County, Pennsylvania, immersing three times forward (trine immersion, as they called it) in the name of the Father, Son, and Holy Ghost, and the River Brethren denomination was started.

The church grew rapidly and spread to surrounding counties. Engle was a forceful evangelist until his death in 1833 at age seventy-nine. During this period the total church took on Pietist leanings. In the 1840s some differences arose, mainly with the York County group, over certain conservative and separate life-style practices. About the same time, in the 1850s, the Dauphin and Lebanon County groups wanted to build meetinghouses, start Sunday Schools, and hold revival meetings which the majority were not ready to accept. The United Zion Churches came out of this division.

In the middle of the Civil War, the larger group which wanted to maintain nonresistance and peace in their basic doctrine, was required to register with the government. For this purpose they needed to choose an official name and they decided on Brethren in Christ. Since that time there have been the three groups: Brethren in Christ, Old Order River Brethren, and United Zion. They meet together every couple of years for an old-fashioned love-feast meal and worship service in a rural barn setting.

Today there are 188 Brethren in Christ congregations in twenty-one states with a total 18,548 membership. Their overseas mission program has been very effective so there are now more members in countries scattered around the world than in North America. Headquarters is located in the village of Grantham, near the Pennsylvania capital of Harrisburg. Their Messiah College is the largest of the Anabaptist colleges with over 2,300 students. Pennsylvania has the highest number of congregations and membership of any state with California in second place. The Brethren in Christ have presently absorbed a blending of Holiness and Wesleyan thought.

The United Zion churches have 856 members in thirteen congregations, all located in Lancaster and Lebanon Counties in Pennsylvania. They maintain a modern retirement and nursing home near Lititz while supporting mission work in Chile, South America.

The Old Order River Brethren have 317 members in five districts located in Iowa and Pennsylvania. There is one small group, called the Old Church, which still uses horse and buggy and all members practice strict separation in dress and life-style.

Church of God in Christ, Mennonite

A remnant, led by John Holdeman, came out of the Mennonite Church between 1859 and the 1880s. During these decades he had much success as an evangelist among the recent immigrations from Poland and Russia. They are frequently referred to as Holdeman Mennonites.

Like some other conservative groups, they do not condone radio or television. The men wear trimmed beards and conventional coats without ties. The women wear modest dresses but no jewelry, and their hair is uncut, pinned under a small black fitted bonnet. For church services their heads are covered with black triangular scarfs. They believe in the doctrine of one true church. They encourage each family unit to limit the size of its agri-business activity to support only themselves.

Church headquarters is in Moundridge, a small town in south-central Kansas. Almost a quarter of the total membership is scattered across this state. There are 107 congregations with about 11,300 members in thirty-three states.

Conservative Mennonite Conference

In the early twentieth century a number of leaders among the Amish Mennonites wanted to hold to some of the positive influences from their Amish backgrounds and did not want to allow centralized power as they perceived to be developing in the Mennonite Church regional conferences. In 1910 they met at Pigeon, Michigan, located in the "thumb" area, where there is now a large congregation as well as several smaller ones in surrounding communities. This Conference was first called Conservative Amish Mennonite but changed to Conservative Mennonite Conference in 1950.

In general, brothers of the rural congregations wear plain coats and sisters wear prayer veilings in their services; however, there is little distinction in the outward appearance of their city and suburban counterparts. They meet in a nationwide conference every August. In recent years they have made a careful and clear statement as to their own identity within the Anabaptist-Mennonite family, based upon the "Authority of the Scriptures." Nonconformity is an important concept in the vocabulary of this group.

Their current outreach efforts have been targeted to the Hispanic population in Sunbelt cities. Denominational headquarters and their very successful Rosedale Bible Institute are both located at Rosedale, Ohio, a small crossroads community near Plain City. They now have 100 congregations with about 9,900 members in nineteen states.

Beachy Amish Mennonite

The reason for the triple title above is a bit complicated. Moses Beachy, an Amish leader in Somerset County in southwestern Pennsylvania, was troubled by the strict shunning practice of the Old Order group. Beachy then became the leader of the one division, which took his name in 1927. About the same time an Amish group in Lancaster County, in the southeastern sector of the state, was struggling with the same problem and joined this new group.

Within the next couple of years they allowed automobiles, trucks, and tractors; built large churches for their growing congregations; started Sunday Schools; and held revival meetings. They encourage evangelical faith and daily discipleship and retain, to this day, a rigid dress code.

There is constant dialogue among them as to the most appropriate name for their group, both local and national. In some communities they call themselves Mennonite; in others, Amish Mennonite; in some, Christian Fellowship; and still others hold to the original Beachy Amish.

They conduct their own parochial schools covering elementary, middle, and high school. A few go on to higher education for specific training in servanthood roles. They sponsor an advanced winter Bible School in Arkansas and hold an annual "Ministers Meeting" which brings together their leadership team of bishops, ministers, and deacons. There is no church headquarters or staff, but their Missions Interest Committee is very active in both domestic and overseas programs. Today there are 102 congregations with 7,400 members in twenty-four states.

Mennonite Christian Fellowship

Early in this decade, this group came out of the Beachy Amish over two issues. First, it insists that all new converts, with focus on the Old Order transfers, must testify to a born-again experience. And second, the name of the group was established to solve the confusion already detailed in the Beachy Amish section.

There are now nineteen congregations with over 1,000 members located in seven states.

Amish Mennonite

This group has assumed its name on a somewhat official nationwide basis. They maintain strong bonds even when scattered from Illinois to Oregon. They also enjoy many family ties and share together in a consistent conservative doctrine and life-style. In these practices they follow the admonition of John Kauffman, known as the "Sleeping Preacher," who often preached while he was in a trance.

There are twelve congregations with about 1,250 members in five states.

Evangelical Mennonite Church

This group has probably moved as far from their Amish roots into Modern Evangelicalism as any Anabaptist-Mennonite subgroup. Most congregations have practically lost any Mennonite identity.

They were first known as the Egly Amish for their leader, Henry Egly. Around 1890 they changed their name to Defenseless Mennonite Church, and in 1948 the name was again changed to Evangelical Mennonite Church.

Headquarters is in Fort Wayne, Indiana. They operate a children's home in Illinois, and their major overseas mission is in the Dominican Republic. They belong to the National Association of Evangelicals. There are twenty-eight congregations with about 4,300 members in six states.

Old Order Mennonites

Today there are about a dozen different groups across the States which assume this category and stand together in their convictions with some distinguishing exceptions. In the 1860s there were serious liberal/conservative discussions among the brethren primarily in the states of Pennsylvania, Ohio, Indiana, and Virginia. Several conservative leaders separated themselves, each with supporters which, in some areas, amounted to a third of the original groups. This withdrawal may have hastened the organizing of various regional groups which became the Old Mennonite Church in the 1890s and, in this century, the Mennonite Church.

During the first decade of this century, serious discussions on theology and life-style were terminated, the break was final, and the Old Order Mennonite Church was organized. Some specific variant points of view were: placement of the pulpit level with the people or on a platform; use of telephones; forms of worship; Sunday Schools, evening meetings, and general church activities; use of the English language for church services; four-part singing; audible prayer versus silent individual prayer; marriage of couples only from within the church by church ministers; and the entanglement by government in settling estates.

The pioneer leaders who led the discussions and held to the more conservative ways were Bishops George Weaver and Jonas Martin in Pennsylvania, Minister Simeon Heatwole in Virginia, and Bishop Jacob Wisler over Ohio and Indiana. There are more than 13,800 members in the Old Order Mennonite family.

Weaverland and
Wisler Mennonite Conferences

These two groups are the only ones in the Old Order lines which permit automobiles. Allowing cars and modern farm equipment since 1927 has brought about a major division among the Old Orders.

They base their doctrine and many church practices on the Dortrecht Confession of Faith, drawn in 1632 in Holland. Their meetinghouses are simple and spartan, and they practice a plain dress code which carries over into homes, furnishings, and general lifestyle. Fellowship and mutuality is very meaningful to them. They maintain an Aid Plan to help their families who suffer from accident, disaster, and long-term health problems resulting in lengthy hospital stays.

They provide their own schools through the eighth grade, cooperating with other Old Order neighbors in some areas. Only acapella singing is used in worship with no instruments permitted. Ministers rely on the guidance of the Spirit for sermons, with minimal or no notes, and much scripture reading. The members hold each other responsible for right living. Farming and associated support to agri-businesses, on a medium scale, are the preferred occupations.

The Weaverland Conference is based in Lancaster County, Pennsylvania; however, they have reached out with new settlements in surrounding counties and into the states of New York, Virginia, Missouri, Iowa, and Wisconsin. They now have thirty-one congregations with over 4,800 members.

Distinctive with the Weaverland Conference, all members drive black vehicles and church leaders have auto bumpers, grilles, and hubcaps painted black. To their neighbors they are known as "black bumper" Mennonites.

The Wisler Conference relates closely to the Weaverland Conference and are found in Ohio, Indiana, and Michigan. Their leaders do not require as strict a separated attitude and life-style. They now have six congregations with a membership of about 670.

Ohio Wisler
Mennonite Group

There are four congregations in eastern Ohio, with a present membership of about 350, divided from the Wisler Conference in 1972. Their leadership allows more acculturation than the parent group. They have started a fifth worship point and are planting another community with the leadership team and lay-families now rotating weekly in support.

Groffdale Old Order
Mennonite Conference

The Groffdale group separated from the Weaverland Conference in 1927, choosing to retain the use of horse and buggy transportation. In some areas they are known as "team" Mennonites. Tractors and modern farm equipment, mounted on steel wheels, are permitted. Most member families pursue farming occupations. They work the "Good Earth" intensely and follow careful conservation measures.

There is some variation of worship forms and practices as established by the bishops, but there are always both an opening and main sermon. As in most Old Order Mennonite groups, the men do not wear beards, but men, women, and children dress modestly and plain. Electricity and telephones are allowed for business purposes. They evaluate in a cautious way any new technology.

In Lancaster County, Pennsylvania, a number of church buildings are shared on alternate Sundays between the Groffdale and Weaverland groups; they visit family or neighboring congregations on the other Sundays.

Pennsylvania has twenty congregations with about 3,300 members. Other states where the Groffdale group has resettled into new communities are New York, Ohio, Kentucky, Missouri, Wisconsin, and Iowa. These six states have fourteen congregations and 1,800 members.

The Indiana Old Order Mennonite Conference joined the Groffdale group about 1970 with five congregations and about 400 members in northern Indiana and southern Michigan.

The Virginia Old Order Mennonite Conference relates very closely to the Groffdale group, having three congregations with over 400 members in and around Dayton. A new settlement is emerging in Washington County in southern Indiana.

Stauffer Old Order Mennonites

As early as the 1840s a young Lancaster Conference ordained minister questioned the authority of the church when two domestic problems were allowed to be taken to public courts, rather than an effort made to resolve them within the church structure. Jacob Stauffer withdrew in 1845 and started his own church, which took his name and was also known locally as Pike Mennonite because the church was located along the pike east of Ephrata.

Their meetinghouses are very plain, with the seating arrangement permitting the audience to face the ministers' table which is along the side of the building and on the same level as the worshippers.

The men have a distinctive haircut and wear a wide-brim black hat. The clothing of the families, their home places, and total living is the plainest of the Mennonite plain groups. Many families make their modest living on forty-to-eighty-acre farmettes and work the fields with horse-drawn implements. Their buggies are very plain and black, and they use only lanterns after dark.

Stauffer published the document, "A Foundation of Faith and Confession," which was the most detailed defense of extreme conservatism written by any American leader or committee until that time. His supporters, then and even today, follow rigid instructions: no worldy offices, meetings, or conventions; no insurance or lightning rods; no attendance at camp meetings or singing schools; no worldly fashions or ornamentation; and no making use of civil courts or force. Scripture is listed to support each statement.

Today there are three Stauffer congregations in Pennsylvania and one each in Maryland, Ohio, Kentucky, and Missouri with a total of 700 members.

Old Order Mennonites, Unaffiliated

This group of fourteen churches is scattered in four states with a total of about 460 members. In general, they are quite exclusive and ultra-conservative. All rely on horses for local travel and farm work. The five congregations in Pennsylvania use the name of their leaders who split from the Stauffer Mennonites. They still share their meetinghouses on alternate Sundays for worship at Ephrata and Port Trevorton.

Four congregations in Tennessee, two in Kentucky, one in Michigan, and another in Maine are independent with localized names. Their leaders are in dialogue with each other, and a degree of fellowship is maintained.

One other small group, the **John Martin Mennonites**, fit into this category. They have two house churches, one in Pennsylvania and another in Missouri, with a combined membership of forty-four.

Please see state listings for other details.

Reidenbach Old Order Mennonites

The "Reidenbachers," as they are called locally, take their name from a very small rural community between Ephrata and Blue Ball in Lancaster County, Pennsylvania. During World War II thirty-five families, clustered in that area, left the Stauffer group. The major issue was whether draft-age men should accept assignment to alternative Civilian Public Service or go to prison for refusal to cooperate with the government for conscience' sake. Several went to prison while others were permitted to remain on farms to produce food.

This group has grown today to a total of about 340 members. The larger communities have meetinghouses while the smaller groups worship as house churches, with ten locations in Pennsylvania, Kentucky, and Missouri.

Wenger/Weaver Old Order Mennonites

Two Wenger congregations near Dayton, Virginia, with Marion Wenger as bishop, and the William Weaver congregation west of Goshen, Indiana, have recently joined in fellowship. Their major difference with the Groffdale Conference is the allowance of their members to have rubber and pneumatic tires on buggies, tractors, and farm machinery. They worship on alternate Sundays in the Groffdale meetinghouses. There are a total of about 320 baptized members.

Noah Hoover Old Order Mennonites

Noah Hoover started his group in the early 1960s. He is still active, residing in their largest community, in south central Kentucky at Scottsville. Total families wear very plain garb and the men wear beards, a custom which is usually associated with the Amish. Noah is a man of deep spirituality, a dedicated Bible student and teacher. He now has several assistants in leadership, with about 220 members in four churches in Kentucky, Pennsylvania, and Missouri.

They mainly grow produce on their farms of minimal acreage, using horse and mule power. In cooperation with some other conservative Mennonite groups, they operate auctions and roadside stands to market their products both wholesale and retail.

New Order Amish

This group started on a very small scale in the early '70s. The value of a personal salvation experience and the introduction of Sunday Schools, Bible Study, chaperoned youth activities, and changes in courting practices were main factors in the formation of the New Order.

They operate many cottage industries. Most New Order districts allow rubber-tired tractors and farm machinery, trucks, and equipment basic to the family business. They utilize horse and buggy transportation for personal travel and church meetings; many services are still held in larger homes, barns, and other buildings, while some are held in meetinghouses.

Today there are forty-four districts with about 2,500 members in eight states, with Ohio having about half of the New Order districts.

Mennonite/Church of the Brethren

Through recent decades these two groups, Mennonite and Church of the Brethren, have come together spontaneously in specific locations. At the denominational level these fellow Anabaptists have cooperated in the production of selected worship books, outreach, and study materials. In the future, with increasing urbanization, church leadership may want to consider a more organized effort to plant such congregations where there is a minimal presence of these two Anabaptist groups. Also, in certain rural communities, these groups may decide to merge, thus strengthening their mission and witness. There are now nine congregations with about 700 members in seven states.

Mennonite Fellowship Churches

Beginning very slowly in the early 1960s without specific leadership, this group is nationwide. The ordained leaders convene in annual conference and all members meet each summer in four regional gatherings. They have about forty-one congregations with over 1,850 members in thirteen states.

As their name implies, sister/brotherhood and fellowship in close community is very important to them. They follow a separated dress code and life-style while also maintaining parochial schools. They have mission outreach in at least six other countries. Tract ministry is an important part of their total program with printing shops in Kentucky, New Mexico, and Pennsylvania.

Conservative Mennonite, Unaffiliated

This group of congregations is not a part of the Conservative Mennonite Conference. However, they include the word Conservative at both congregational and denominational levels. Members practice conservative concerns and life-style and, in some cases, follow a conservative leader. They prefer to maintain a degree of independence.

There are thirteen congregations with about 900 members in six states. Ohio claims the most members.

Reformed Mennonites and United Mennonites

The first major division over doctrinal issues for Mennonites in the states occurred in 1812. Until that time geographical lines defined the various groups. John Herr (1781-1850) believed he received a vision in which Christ told him to organize a new church because the Mennonite Church was departing from the teachings of Menno Simons. At first his followers were called New Mennonites; later they chose the title Reformed.

Herr traveled by horseback from Strasburg in Lancaster County to surrounding communities and counties in Pennsylvania, as far west as Illinois and north into New York and Ontario, winning converts and starting churches. At one time there were almost 3,000 members in about thirty congregations in Ontario and eight states. Today there are less than 300 members in four states with eight congregations.

In the 1930s an influential Afro-American woman became convinced of the Reformed Way by reading some of their writings. A small group in Oakland, Tennessee, a town just east of Memphis, now continues a house church relationship. Ministers from the congregations in the central states serve them.

The male members are identified by their plain coats, small bow ties, and derby-style hats. Women wear full bonnets, shawls, and long cape dresses with matching aprons in various shades of gray.

In 1975 Minister Willis Weaver was expelled for criticism of the Reformed leaders. With a few followers he organized the United Mennonite Church which today worships in homes with about a dozen members. At a 1995 inter-Mennonite meeting in Lancaster County, one brother observed, "The United Mennonites may be our smallest group."

Evangelical Mennonite Brethren

During the decade of the 1980s, this group changed its name to Fellowship of Evangelical Bible Churches. However, four congregations, with about 500 members, chose to retain the former name. Those are located in Kansas, Minnesota, Montana, and South Dakota.

Amish Mennonite, Unaffiliated

This group follows in general the conservative theology and life-style of the several branches described earlier, but in a few cases the congregational leadership tends to be more conservative. There are eight congregations with over 300 members, mostly clustered in Kentucky and Tennessee.

Anabaptist Christian Fellowship

In 1982 several familes from Old Order and Beachy Amish backgrounds in Lancaster County, Pennsylvania, formed this group in an effort to reclaim the main tenets of Anabaptist faith as they understood them. They were interested in more congregationalism and less denominationalism. Through the years ministers and laity from non-Anabaptist groups have joined this fellowship. Most sisters wear a distinctive kerchief/scarf head covering.

Today there are nineteen congregations in twelve states with 973 members. From their base at Charity Fellowship in Leola they distribute a tape ministry and some home schooling materials to a wide following. In the recent decade this group has the largest percentage of growth in both congregations and membership of any Anabaptist-Mennonite group.

Old Colony Mennonite

Coming out of Canada and Mexico, this group settled in Seminole, West Texas, in the recent '70s. They also have constituents on immigrant labor status who follow the planting and harvest cycles into central California, northcentral Iowa, and southwest Kansas. Services are provided by their own leadership once monthly, in season. There are 340 adult baptized members in the established Seminole community.

Reinlaender Mennonite

With a membership of about 170, this group is also settled in Seminole, Texas, and has come out of Mexico and Canada. They have simpler homes, church, and school facilities, and live a more spartan life-style, across the main highway from the Old Colony families, southeast of Seminole.

Mennonite Evangelical Churches

The name for this group, coming out of western Canada, was first known as Evangelical Mennonite Conference (EMC). In the States they recently changed their name, as titled above. They have congregations in Paris and Seminole, Texas, and a school and church in Copeland and Montezuma, Kansas. They have a total of 208 members.

Evangelical Mennonite Mission Conference

Evangelical Mennonite Mission Conference (EMMC) is based in Winnipeg, Manitoba. They have only one outreach congregation in the States, located at Seminole, Texas, with about 150 members. As the name implies, they are of evangelical thought and are mission minded.

Kleine Gemeinde Community

Translated from the German these words mean "Little Church." This group came from Mexico more than twenty years ago and resettled into a solid community near Boley, in central Oklahoma. They operate their own school in their church building. They have sixty-five adult members.

General Conference, Mennonite Brethren, Mennonite Church

This one "tri-conference" congregation is located in Manhatten, Kansas. The university setting brings faculty, staff, and students together. There are sixty adult members in the Manhatten Mennonite Church.

Mennonite Brethren/Mennonite Church

This "one-of-a-kind" congregation is located in rural southeast Texas and involved in agri-business activities. There are thirty-five members in the United Mennonite Church at Premont.

Mennonite Church/Other Denominations

There are three congregations, one each in Arizona, Colorado, and New York with this unusual arrangement. Please check the state listings for additional information. The total membership stands at about 160.

Where We Are

[State Statistics and Summaries From Largest To Smallest]

		Congregations Districts Fellowships	Baptized Membership
1.	Pennsylvania	886	87,177
2.	Ohio	498	40,726
3.	Indiana	351	29,654
4.	Kansas	117	21,570
5.	California	110	12,869
6.	Illinois	114	10,239
7.	Virginia	107	10,228
8.	Michigan	130	7,420
9.	New York	99	6,449
10.	Iowa	73	6,160
11.	Missouri	83	5,835
12.	Oklahoma	51	5,316
13.	Wisconsin	94	5,206
14.	Oregon	49	5,143
15.	Florida	61	4,887
16.	Maryland	62	4,462
17.	South Dakota	26	3,694
18.	Kentucky	71	3,523
19.	Nebraska	23	3,506
20.	Minnesota	43	3,227
21.	Washington	19	3,067
22.	Texas	47	2,779
23.	Colorado	31	1,904

24.	Tennessee	38	1,723
25.	Mississippi	23	1,620
26.	Arizona	28	1,443
27.	Delaware	17	1,344
28.	Idaho	13	1,194
29.	Georgia	22	1,148
30.	North Carolina	27	1,088
31.	Montana	19	859
32.	Alabama	16	838
33.	Arkansas	17	745
34.	Puerto Rico	18	684
35.	North Dakota	12	646
36.	Louisiana	6	609
37.	South Carolina	10	590
38.	New Jersey	14	587
39.	West Virginia	16	442
40.	New Mexico	12	428
41.	District of Columbia	5	322
42.	Massachusetts	4	273
43.	Connecticut	3	202
44.	Vermont	5	200
45.	Maine	5	98
46.	Hawaii	2	78
47.	Wyoming	1	17
48.	Alaska	1	9

1. Pennsylvania

This state has thirty-one subgroups; 886 congregations, districts, and fellowships; and a baptized membership of 87,177, making it number one across the nation. The largest group is the Mennonite Church, relating to six conferences with 32,100 members. Next is the Old Order Amish with about 15,000, and third is the Brethren in Christ with 12,500 members. Lancaster City and

County, located in the southeast sector, is the "Jerusalem" for the state, with about thirty churches having a city address and another 270 with county addresses. Lancaster Conference is the largest in the Mennonite Church.

Philadelphia, where the first Mennonites landed in 1683 from Europe, now has about twenty churches with a large multicultural ratio. To the north of the city in Montgomery County and neighboring counties, there are several clusters of congregations of various groups around Bethlehem, Quakertown, and Souderton.

Other concentrations are in Chambersburg and Franklin County to the west along the Maryland state line, and further into Somerset County, north to Johnstown, named for an early Amish leader, and on to the northwest counties of the state.

For the General Conference Mennonites, Pennsylvania is the second largest state with about 4,500 members living mainly in the southeastern counties. The Brethren in Christ are centered around the state capital of Harrisburg.

This state also has the largest communities of both Old Order Amish and Mennonites. They have spread from two bases, Lancaster County and Big Valley near Lewistown, into surrounding counties with strong settlements to the north and west along the New York and Ohio state borders. In the Lancaster/Chester area the gray buggies belong to the Amish and the black buggies, to the "team" Mennonites. In the Big Valley the black buggies belong to the Renno Amish; the yellow top buggies belong to the Byler Group; and the light brown with white tops, to the Nebraska group. This group came from the state of Nebraska years ago when they were forced from there by intense and long-term drought conditions.

Mennonite Church independent conferences and unaffiliated congregations have their largest membership in this state with approximately 5,200 and 1,250 each. A majority follow a plain clothing and life-style code. The Amish and Old Order Mennonites wear mostly solid dark colors, but the men wear traditional white shirts and the women, white aprons.

About a third of the total nationwide Anabaptist-Mennonite membership is clustered in the Keystone State. The smallest subgroup in the state is the United Mennonite house meeting with a dozen members in the Lancaster area.

2. Ohio

The State of Ohio has twenty-six subgroups and 498 congregations, districts, and fellowships, with over 40,700 baptized members.

Groups with the largest membership are: first, the Old Order Amish districts with about 13,000; second, the Ohio Mennonite Church conference congregations with 10,200; and third, the conservative Mennonite conference with over 3,300 members.

Holmes and Wayne Counties claim the largest concentration of Amish and Mennonites. The "horse-and-buggy" groups are scattered in large communities and smaller settlements all over the state. There is good representation in the cities, their suburbs, and surrounding areas. Canton has at least five congregations and districts while Akron, Cincinnati, Cleveland, Columbus, Dayton, Lima, Toledo, and Youngstown each have one or more.

Just east of Cleveland, in Geauga County, there is a large settlement of Amish and several brands of Amish/Mennonite and Mennonite. In Parma, just south of Cleveland, a 500-member Russian Evangelical congregation has recently joined the Mennonite Brethren. Afro-American congregations are located in Cleveland and Youngstown, while Hispanic congregations are found in the northwest section of the state. Also, to the northwest, around the towns of Archbold and Wauseon, there is a concentration of Mennonite communities with members heavily involved in progressive agricultural, commercial, industrial, and professional pursuits.

Congregations are found in many small cities, towns, and villages across the Buckeye State. The first Mennonite Sunday School in the state was introduced at West Liberty where there are now three congregations and a fellowship. Also, a special education residential school which developed out of an earlier orphanage and children's home is located there.

The Brethren in Christ are located in the northeast and southwest portions of the state. The office for the Ohio Mennonite Conference, formed in 1824, is located in the Swiss village of Kidron. There is a cluster of General Conference Mennonite congregations around their Bluffton College between Lima and Toledo.

The smallest group in the state is the Stauffer Old Order Mennonite community at Bainbridge, near Chillicothe, with eighteen members.

3. Indiana

The Hoosier State has twenty subgroups in 351 districts, congregations, and fellowships with a total of over 29,650 baptized members.

The Old Order Amish can count about 11,200 members, the Mennonite Church Conference membership adds up to more than 9,700, and the General Conference Mennonite Church is third with over 2,200 members. The offices for the state Mennonite Church conference, formed in 1824, and the district covering several states for the General Conference Mennonites are both located in Goshen.

Menno's followers are primarily clustered together in Elkhart and Lagrange Counties in the northern part of the state. There are about forty congregations, districts, and fellowships with a Goshen address. Elkhart has ten congregations. Old Order and other branches of Amish and Mennonites are settled in or near the towns of Bristol, Howe, Lagrange, Ligonier, Middlebury, Millersburg, Nappanee, New Paris, Shipshewana, Topeka, Wakarusa, and Wolcottville. Goshen College, with an enrollment of 1,100 students, is sponsored by the Mennonite Church. The Brethren in Christ operate a publishing house at Nappanee.

In the Fort Wayne area there are about twenty-five congregations and districts. Two congregations are in the capital city of Indianapolis and in South Bend with fellowships in Bloomington, Evansville, and West Lafayette. In the rural counties of Adams and Daviess and small towns of Berne, Geneva, Loogootee, Montgomery, and Tippecanoe, as well as the small cities of Kokomo, Muncie, Rensselaer, Valparaiso, and Washington, one will find communities of conservative and plain folks along with contemporary congregations.

The smallest group in the state is a Dual Conference Mennonite/Church of the Brethren Hispanic congregation in South Bend.

4. Kansas

The state of Kansas has fifteen subgroups with 117 congregations, districts, and fellowships having 21,570 baptized members.

The General Conference Mennonite Church is the largest in the state with thirty-five congregations and about 9,000 members. Second is the Church of God in Christ, Mennonite with twenty-three congregations and 3,550 members, and a near third is the Mennonite Brethren with fifteen congregations and a membership of 3,520. The western district office of the GCs is in North Newton while the southern district office of the MBs is in Wichita, each covering several surrounding states. The South Central Conference of the MCs, founded in 1876, also maintains an office in North Newton and covers neighboring states.

The inter-Mennonite population is centered in Newton, Harvey County, and the surrounding counties. There is a chain of communities and congregations stretching across the prairies to the west and southwest with Garden City, Greensburg, Hays, Liberal, Meade, Montezuma, Protection, and Ulysses as anchors. Congregations are established in Kansas City and suburbs, Topeka, and Wichita. Fellowships and congregations are found in Hutchinson, Lawrence, Manhattan, McPherson, Olathe, and Salina. The Amish and Plain People are clustered around Garnett, Haven, Partridge, and Yoder. The Brethren in Christ have settled in and around historic Abilene.

There is a junior college at Hesston and senior colleges, Tabor and Bethel, at Hillsboro and North Newton. Kansas has the largest membership of both dual conference and independent Mennonite congregations, each group with over 1,000 members.

The smallest group in the state is a single congregation of the Mennonite Evangelical Church with sixteen members at Montezuma.

5. California

The Golden State of California has five subgroups with 110 congregations and fellowships having about 12,900 members. It is fifth in line of state Anabaptist-Mennonite population.

Mennonite Brethren have the largest membership with 8,400; second is the Pacific Southwest Conference, a merger in 1994 of the General Conference Mennonite and Mennonite Church with 2,100 members; and third is the Brethren in Christ numbering 1,500 members. Other groups are the Church of God in Christ, Mennonite, with about 770 members, and three new congregations of the

Mennonite Fellowship Churches, and the smallest, the Mennonite Christian Fellowship at Beckwourth in the northern sector of the state. The first organized group in the state was the former General Conference Mennonite Pacific District which formed in 1896.

The Mennonite Brethren are centered in the rich agricultural area of the San Joaquin Valley and cities of Bakersfield, Fresno, and Reedley. A majority of the southwest Pacific Mennonite Conference churches are found in the Los Angeles metropolitan area while the Brethren in Christ center is in Upland, sixty miles to the east. However, congregations and fellowships of the several groups stretch from the capital city of Sacramento, San Francisco, and San Jose to San Diego.

California has assimilated many immigrant groups in recent decades, reflected in the multi-cultured Mennonite statewide community. The large Mennonite Brethren constituency can be divided into at least ten different ethnic groups. They list fourteen Latino congregations. The Mennonite Pacific Southwest Conference has a number of African-American, Hispanic, Indonesian, and Asian churches.

The Pacific District office of the MBs is on the campus of their Fresno Pacific College, graduate school, and seminary. The offices for the Pacific Southwest Mennonite Conference, covering the northern sector of the state, are located at Clovis and, in the southern sector, at Downey. The bishop's office for the Midwest and Pacific area conferences of the Brethren in Christ is in Upland.

6. Illinois

Sixteen subgroups of Anabaptist-Mennonites have scattered in all directions within Illinois. They now have 114 congregations, districts, and fellowships, with over 10,200 members.

The largest group here is the Illinois Mennonite Church Conference with about 3,700 members. The second is the General Conference Mennonite with about 1,600 members, and third is the Old Order Amish districts with 1,485 membership.

A majority of the communities are settled in the rich agricultural area between Bloomington/Normal and Peoria, and northward. In fact, Peoria and surrounding communities have about a dozen congregations. Several congregations are in the Bloomington/ Normal area, and a large Mennonite-operated hospital is located there.

The Amish and Conservative Mennonites are centered around the town of Arthur in the central/east area. But both groups are opening new districts and establishing new congregations to the west and south sectors of the state.

ChicagoLand Anabaptist/Mennonites are growing in number with about twenty congregations and a good representation of Afro-American and Hispanic congregations. Other cities where congregations are now located are Champaign/Urbana, Freeport, Kankakee, Moline, and Sterling. The largest Mennonite/Church of the Brethren congregation, nationwide, is in Evanston. The Illinois Mennonite Church Conference was organized in 1872, and the office is now located in Bradley. There is no congregation in the capital city of Springfield. The smallest subgroup in the state is an eleven-member Mennonite Brethren congregation in Chicago.

It is interesting to note between these two states the close total membership of 10,239 for Illinois, and 10,228 for Virginia. I predict that Virginia may go around Illinois in the near future. In recent years Virginia Anabaptist-Mennonite population has grown at an approximate annual rate of nine percent, while Illinois is growing at the rate of three percent.

---

7. Virginia

The state of Virginia can count thirteen groups of Anabaptist Mennonites with 108 congregations, districts, and fellowships, and a total of over 10,200 members. The Virginia Mennonite Church Conference is the largest with 6,300 members, and the Cornerstone Independent District is second with over 1,000 members, while the Independent Southeastern Conference is third with 650 members.

Harrisonburg is the "Jerusalem" city with fifteen congregations, a parochial elementary, middle, and high school; university; and seminary. Also located there are a retirement and nursing center, the Virginia Mennonite Conference office, and national Mennonite Media Ministries headquarters.

Congregations are clustered up and down the beautiful Shenandoah Valley. The Old Order Mennonite groups are centered around the town of Dayton. Several congregations are located in the northern Virginia suburbs of the nation's capital. About ten congregations are found in the Eastern Shore cities of Chesapeake, Hampton, Newport News, Norfolk, Virginia Beach, and Williamsburg.

Four congregations are established in the state capital of Richmond. Other congregations and fellowships are scattered in the rural hills and vales, small towns and villages, and the cities of Charlottesville, Christiansburg, Fredericksburg, Lynchburg, Roanoke, and Winchester. The smallest is the twenty-six-member Dual Conference (GC/MC) fellowship in Richmond.

The Old Order Amish in recent years have returned to the state, and now have settlements in Abingdon, Burkes Garden, and southwest of Pearisburg.

8. Michigan

The state of Michigan can list eighteen different Anabaptist-Mennonite groups with 131 congregations, districts, and fellowships, having a total membership of 7,450. The branch office of the Indiana/Michigan Conference of the Mennonite Church is in Mancelona.

The largest group is the Old Order Amish with about 2,900 members. Next is the Mennonite Church Conference with over 2,200 members, and third is the Conservative Mennonite Conference with 655 members. The state has a number of denominational church camps and retreat centers.

There are about a dozen congregations in the Upper Peninsula. Some fifty congregations and districts have moved over the state lines from Indiana and Ohio into communities in the southern counties. There is a distribution of communities and settlements from central to northern sectors of the state, and northeast into the Thumb Area. Many families depend on agri-business activities for their living.

The city of Detroit has two Afro-American congregations, as does Saginaw. There is also a fellowship in Detroit, two in Ann Arbor, and another in East Lansing. Other cities with congregations are Battle Creek, Flint, Midland, Petoskey, and Traverse City. A large number of congregations are in small towns and rural settings. A church in Grand Rapids closed in recent years.

9. New York

New York State has listed fifteen subgroups of Anabaptist-Mennonites with ninety-nine congregations, districts, and fellowships, and about 6,450 in membership.

The largest group is the Mennonite Church with four conferences covering the state with a total membership of about 1,800. The largest conference is the New York Conference, established in 1973, with about 1,175 members, and an office at Martinsburg. The Old Order Amish districts have about 1,700 baptized members. The Conservative Mennonite Conference, clustered in upstate New York and numbering 1,050 members, is in third place. There is a retirement center and nursing home located at Lowville.

The Mennonite Church Conference congregations are clustered in three areas: in and around New York City, east of Buffalo, and near the Pennsylvania line from Corning/Elmira westward. The Amish are settled in large communities in the southwest sector of the state, migrating from Ohio, and also scattered into other counties across the state. The "team" Mennonites and other ultra-conservative groups have resettled into the fertile Finger Lakes region.

The boroughs and suburbs of New York City can count over twenty Afro-American and Hispanic congregations and fellowships. Some are small with a dozen or so members, while others have a membership of upwards to 120.

There are also other cultural and ethnic groups with a variety of ministries. There is a dual denominational Mennonite/Elim Fellowship congregation, called Immanuel, at Flushing.

Additional cities with congregations or fellowships are Buffalo, Corning, Rochester, Syracuse, and Watertown. There is no Anabaptist-Mennonite presence in the capital city of Albany or on Long Island.

The smallest subgroup in the state is the "Holdeman" Mennonites with recent outreach into both the Finger Lakes region and New York City.

10. Iowa

Iowa ranks as the tenth state in Anabaptist-Mennonite population with 6,160 in seventy-three congregations, districts, and fellowships. There are fourteen different subgroups.

The largest group is the Iowa-Nebraska Mennonite Church Conference with about 2,850 members, and then the Old Order Amish with over 1,700 members, followed by the General Conference Mennonites with a membership of 500-plus.

Large percentages of both Amish and Mennonites are settled in the southeastern counties and villages of Kalona, Keota, Washington, Wayland, and Wellman. The Old Order car and team Mennonites are purchasing land and building new farming communities around Charles City in the northeast sector. Other scattered towns where our people are located are Bloomfield, Dallas Center, Hazleton, Leon, Manson, and Milton. Cities where congregations and fellowships are located are the capital city of Des Moines, and Ames, Burlington, Davenport, Fort Dodge, Iowa City, Muscataine, and Cedar Falls/Waterloo. There are two Hispanic congregations in the state.

Corn and pork are major products from the small and large farms of the statewide sister/brotherhood. The smallest group in the state is the Old Order Weaverland Conference community at Nora Springs.

11. Missouri

The total Anabaptist-Mennonite membership is about 5,850 for Missouri with nineteen subgroups in eighty-three congregations, districts, and fellowships.

The Old Order Amish, with 2,100 baptized members, is the largest group of Anabaptists settled across the state with concentrations at Clark, Jamesport, and Seymour. The Mennonite Church Conference congregations can count over 600 members in their communities in and around historic Hannibal in the northeast sector, and at Garden City and Harrisonville just south of Kansas City. The Amish Mennonite congregations at Buffalo, Sedalia, and Vandalia add up to 535.

The Amish continue to resettle in Missouri, increasing their districts. The Old Order car and team Mennonites are concentrated in four communities: around Versailles just west of the state capital Jefferson City, near Memphis in the northeast corner of the state, and at Rich Hill and Tunas. There are now nine congregations with eight different kinds of Menno-followers surrounding Versailles.

Saint Louis has two Afro-American congregations in the city and a Dual Conference congregation in the suburbs. A high percentage of the brotherhood across the state are with the various plain groups. The two smallest groups are the Mennonite/Church of the Brethren fellowship at Columbia and the Old Order John Martin house church at Barnett, each with about ten members. Metro Kansas City at one time had a Mennonite city mission and a fellowship in the suburbs but has no such active group at the present time.

12. Oklahoma

The Sooner State has over 5,300 membership, in fifty-one congregations, districts, and fellowships, from nine subgroups of Anabaptist-Mennonites. The Mennonite Brethren congregations total about 2,600 members with the larger ones at Collinsville, Corn, and Fairview. The General Conference Mennonites total about 1,200 members, and the Church of God in Christ, Mennonites have about 450 members.

There is a distribution of communities from the southwest sector, to the western counties, into the northwest and Panhandle section, and across the northern sector to the northeast counties, in and near smaller towns. But only the Old Order Amish has a district in the southeast sector between Clarita and Coalgate.

Oklahoma City, in the very center of the state, and its suburbs claim several congregations. Tulsa has one congregation, and the towns to the east, Adair, Chouteau, Inola, and Pryor, have a network of communities. Other cities with a congregation or fellowship are Broken Arrow, Chichasha, Clinton, Enid, Lawton, Stillwater, and Weatherford. Other towns with congregations in or near are Boley, Cordell, Hydro, and Thomas.

There are several Native American congregations in the state. The smallest is a new church of the Unaffiliated Conservative Mennonite group at Paden.

13. Wisconsin

Wisconsin is often called the Dairyland State, and many Amish/Mennonite family units are involved in dairy farm operations and cheese-making. There are fourteen subgroups across the state with ninety-four congregations, districts, and fellowships. A high percentage can be identified as conservative, Old Order, and plain. The total membership is over 5,200 with perhaps less than ten percent conforming to a contemporary life-style.

The largest group in the state is the Old Order Amish with over 3,500 members. Next is the Church of God in Christ, Mennonites with 390 members, and third are the Mennonite Fellowship Churches with about 300 members.

There are small congregations in Madison and Sheboygan, and two in Waukesha, a suburb of Milwaukee. Then the communities and settlements are scattered into all sections of small towns and rural counties all over the state map. The smallest subgroup is Unaffiliated Conservative Mennonites, with about forty members at Sheldon.

14. Oregon

The state of Oregon is like most other Pacific and Rocky Mountain states with fewer subgroups. Here there are seven with forty-nine congregations and fellowships having a total of about 5,200 members.

The largest group is the Pacific Northwest Dual Conference congregations with over 2,200 members. Next are the Mennonite Brethren with about 1,500 members and third is the Unaffiliated Mennonite Church congregations with 750 members.

A large majority of the communities and congregations are settled in the fertile Willamette Valley. One congregation is in the far eastern sector at La Grande, one is in the central sector near Redmond, and two are at Logsden and Toledo near the Pacific Coast.

The metropolitan area of Portland and the capital city of Salem each has a half-dozen congregations. The cities of Corvallis, Eugene, and Grants Pass to the south, each have two congregations. There are now several Hispanic and Slavic/Ukranian congregations.

The smallest group is the Amish Mennonites with a congregation of about ninety at Harrisburg.

15. Florida

The Sunshine State has nine Anabaptist-Mennonite groups with sixty-one congregations, districts, and fellowships, and about 4,900 baptized members.

The Mennonite Church Conferences, Southeast and Lancaster, have the largest number, about 2,450. The Brethren in Christ are second with over 1,000 members, and the Conservative Mennonite Conference is third with over 650 members.

Southeast Mennonite Conference was formed in 1978 with its office and staff at Sarasota. The Lancaster Conference has a number of small congregations in the western Panhandle. The Brethren in Christ have a large cluster of Cuban congregations and the Mennonite Church has Afro-American, Haitian, and Spanish congregations in the Greater Miami Area.

Sarasota is the "Jerusalem" site in the state with fifteen inter-Mennonite, Amish, and Brethren in Christ congregations and about 2,450 members. There is a large denominational retirement center and nursing home known as Sunnyside Village. The Amish began coming to Sarasota in the late '20s, the Mennonites in the early '30s, and the Brethren in Christ in the mid-'50s.

Clearwater, Saint Petersburg, and Tampa have a number of multi-cultural congregations, while Greater Orlando has three. Tallahasee has one congregation, and Blountstown to the west has several small congregations. A larger Church of God in Christ, Mennonite congregation is located in the very northwest corner of the Panhandle at Walnut Hill. Cape Coral has a growing congregation and Fort Myers has a Spanish-speaking congregation. There are no congregations along the Gold East Coast.

The smallest group is the Hispanic Dual Conference congregation in Miami, Encuentro de Renovacion, with forty members.

16. Maryland

The State of Maryland has thirteen subgroups with sixty-two congregations, districts, and fellowships totaling 4,450 members. The Mennonite Church Conferences number over 1,350 while the

Independent Mennonite Conferences count about 1,300 members and the Old Order Amish districts total 400 members.

Hagerstown and surrounding communities claim a center with over a dozen congregations and fellowships. There are several congregations in and around the city of Baltimore and also a number in the suburbs contiguous to Washington, D.C. There are communities scattered from the eastern shore to the western mountains, from Ocean City, Salisbury, and Westover, across the Chesapeake Bay to Charlotte Hill, Loveville, and Mechanicsville, and out to Flintstone, Cumberland, Pinto, and Grantsville, and down again to Accident and Oakland.

About half of Menno's adherents in the state follow a separated dress code and life-style. Brook Lane mental hospital is located near Hagerstown. The smallest congregation is the Mennonite/Church of the Brethren Gortner Union Fellowship with ten members.

17. South Dakota

South Dakota has about 3,700 members of Anabaptist-Mennonites in twenty-six congregations and fellowships representing six subgroups. The largest group is the General Conference Mennonites with about 1,800 members, then the Mennonite Brethren with over 1,100, and the Independent Mennonite congregations are third with about 550 members.

Freeman, in the southeast sector of the state, is the central town for a majority of members. It is home for a Mennonite Academy and the Northern District office for the General Conference Mennonites. Sioux Falls has three congregations. There is a fellowship in Brookings and a congregation at Huron plus several in nearby rural areas. To the center of the state there are congregations at Gettysburg and Onida.

In the southwest, Rapid City now has a congregation which developed from the Mennonite Disaster Service project after an intense 1972 flash flood. There are also Native Sioux congregations at Pine Ridge and Porcupine. The smallest groups are the Church of God in Christ, Mennonite at Iroquois and the Evangelical Mennonite Brethren at Marion.

18. Kentucky

The Anabaptist-Mennonite membership in this state is distributed between nineteen subgroups with seventy-two districts, congregations, and fellowships having a total of about 3,525 baptized members. In recent years many of the Old Order and ultra-conservative groups have resettled into communities across the state map.

The Old Order Amish add up to about 1,210, then the Beachy Amish Mennonites with over 400 members, and third are the New Order Amish totaling about 250.

The two largest cities, Lexington and Louisville, each have a congregation planted by the Conservative Mennonite Conference. There are seven different kinds of Amish which have established districts from the central section of the state and to the southern and western counties. And there are five different kinds of Old Order Mennonites, also in the southern and western counties. Then there are another five different, conservative, and plain Mennonite groups with about a dozen congregations scattered from the central Bluegrass section into the eastern Appalachia counties. There is a cluster of Brethren in Christ congregations around Campbellsville and Columbia.

The smallest group and congregation is the Unaffiliated Mennonite Church at Wild Cat near Manchester.

19. Nebraska

The state of Nebraska counts six subgroups of Anabaptist-Mennonites, with twenty-three congregations and fellowships and a total of about 3,500 members. The largest group is the General Conference Mennonites with 1,500 members, then the Mennonite Church Conference numbering around 1,200, and the Mennonite Brethren with 435 members.

The concentration of members is in and around the two rural communities of Henderson and Milford. The office of the Iowa-Nebraska Conference of the Mennonite Church, organized in 1920, is located at Milford.

The city of Omaha can now count five congregations with both Afro-American and Hispanic representation. The capital city of Lincoln has a Dual-Conference congregation.

To the southeast of the state one will find Mennonites at Beatrice and Shickley; to the northeast, at Beemer; in the central part, at Broken Bow, Cairo, Greeley, and Wood River; and to the west, at Grant and Madrid.

The smallest group is the fifty-eight-member Unaffiliated Mennonite congregation at Beaver Crossing.

20. Minnesota

Eleven Anabaptist-Mennonite subgroups with forty-three congregations, districts, and fellowships numbering 3,227 members are found in Minnesota.

The General Conference Mennonites add up to over 1,100 members. Next is the Old Order Amish with 715 and third are the Mennonite Brethren with 590.

The twin cities of Minneapolis/Saint Paul and their suburbs have ten congregations. Mountain Lake, a town in the southwest part of the state, claims ten congregations in the area. Duluth, International Falls, and Rochester each have fellowships. The Old Order Amish and the Beachy Amish have resettled into central, western, and southern counties. Conservative Mennonites have settled in small communities across the northern counties. There are HMONG, Lao Christian, and Russian Evangelical congregations in the state which relate to Mennonite groups.

The Unaffiliated Black River Mennonite congregation at Loman, near the Red Lake Indian Reservation, is the smallest group in the state.

21. Washington

The state of Washington has only four groups of Anabaptist-Mennonites in nineteen congregations and fellowships with a total of over 3,050 members.

The Mennonite Brethren group is the largest with about 2,480 members, over half in Slavic/Ukranian congregations. Next are the Dual Conference (GC/MC) Pacific Northwest congregations with about 500 members, third is the Church of God in Christ, Mennonites with about eighty members, and the smallest is the

Independent Conference Mennonite congregation in Colville Valley with about ten members.

The concentration is along the Puget Sound area on the west side of the state in the cities of Bellingham and Seattle with their suburbs, adding up to eight congregations. One congregation is at Vancouver across the Columbia River from Portland, Oregon. There are five congregations in the central agricultural counties at Ephrata, Othello, Ritzville, Tonasket, and Warden, two in the eastern city of Spokane, and one in the town of Newport. There is no representation in the capital city of Tacoma.

22. Texas

The largest state in the Union has fifteen subgroups, forty-seven congregations, districts, and fellowships with a total of about 2,800 baptized Anabaptist-Mennonites.

The Church of God in Christ, Mennonites (Holdeman) have eight congregations with over 550 members, and the Mennonite Church Conference (South Central) has nine congregations and 480 members. The Old Colony Mennonite community at Seminole which has about 350 members is third.

There are six congregations in the Dallas/Fort Worth complex; San Antonio has three while Houston and the capital city of Austin each have one.

Four congregations are found in the Panhandle while in the western sector at Seminole there are also four. In the Rio Grande Valley, from Laredo to Brownsville, there is a concentration of fifteen mostly Spanish-speaking congregations.

Several congregations are clustered in and around Corpus Christi while to the northeast a couple are located near Paris. Smaller cities and towns where Anabaptist-Mennonites are settled include Canton, El Campo, Lott, Victoria, and in Scurry County.

The smallest group is the Old Order Amish district at Gonzales with thirteen members.

23. Colorado

Colorado has ten groups of Anabaptist-Mennonites with thirty-one congregations and fellowships having 1,900 baptized members. The largest group is the Mennonite Church Rocky Mountain Conference with about 1,150 members which was formed in 1961 with an office now at Monument. Next are the Dual Conference congregations with over 200 members. The smallest is the Anabaptist Christian Fellowship at Bellvue with eighteen members.

There are seven congregations in the Denver Metropolitan area, and four in the Colorado Springs area. Reaching north and east there are congregations in Boulder, Fort Collins, Greeley, and Julesburg while to the central east one will find small congregations at Limon and Vona. In the rich southeast irrigated agricultural and ranch lands communities have been established for generations at Cheraw, La Junta, and Rocky Ford.

To the south, congregations are located at Pueblo and Walsenburg. A United Mennonite/Presbyterian congregation is at La Jara. On the southwestern slopes several plain groups have re-settled around Montrose. On the western range congregations are active in Glenwood Springs and around Grand Junction.

24. Tennessee

The Volunteer State can now count ten subgroups of Anabaptist-Mennonites with thirty-eight congregations and districts and about 1,750 adult baptized members.

The largest group is the Old Order Amish with about 500 members, then the Beachy Amish Mennonites numbering about 225, and the Brethren in Christ counting a membership of about 200 members.

There is one congregation in the Nashville area, two in Knoxville, but none in any other major city such as Chattanooga or Memphis. The Old Order Amish began settling in Tennessee in the 1950s and are now clustered around Bruceton and Ethridge. All other communities and congregations are scattered from the eastern mountain ranges to western flatlands, and are also dotted here and there, north to south.

Towns with communities, congregations, and districts in or near them are Belvidere, Cookeville, Cottage Grove, Crossville, DeRossett, Finger, Greeneville, Lewisburg, Lobelville, Monterey,

Mountain City, Sparta, Whitesville, and Woodbury. The Reformed Mennonite House Church at Oakland is the smallest group with nine members.

25. Mississippi

There are six Anabaptist-Mennonite subgroups, with twenty-three congregations, districts, and fellowships, and 1,620 members in the state of Mississippi. The largest group is the Church of God in Christ, Mennonite with over 850 members, and then the Mennonite Church Conference congregations with 400 members. The smallest group is the Mennonite Independent Conference congregation at Darbun with twenty-four members.

Macon, in the eastern sector, is the center for a number of congregations. There is an Afro-American congregation in the capital city of Jackson with the appropriate name, Open Door. There are three Choctaw Native American congregations in the central section of the state. Congregations are scattered from the southern cities of Gulfport and Meridian, northwest to Clarksdale and Leland, and northeast to Aberdeen.

In fact, Mississippi ranks twenty-fifth in chronological order of membership in the total listing of states.

26. Arizona

In Arizona there are eight Anabaptist-Mennonite subgroups with twenty-eight congregations and fellowships, and about 1,450 total statewide membership. The largest group is the dual conference congregations of the Pacific Southwest Mennonite Conference which totals about 1,000 members. The next two groups, Church of God in Christ, Mennonite and Conservative Mennonite Conference, can count about 150 and 140 members each.

There is a concentration of about fifteen congregations in the Greater Phoenix Area. The first Mennonites to relocate to the state arrived in the early forties of this century for health reasons. Tucson, Prescott, Wickenburg, and Willcox each claim a congregation. To the northeast sector of the state about a dozen small congregations are ministering in scattered Native reservation settings. There are a couple active Spanish congregations. The smallest group is an American Baptist/Mennonite Church in the community of Hotevilla on the Navajo reservation.

27. Delaware

There are four subgroups, seventeen congregations and districts, and a total of over 1,300 Anabaptist-Mennonites in the state of Delaware. The Conservative Mennonite Conference is the largest group with 600 members. Next is the Old Order Amish districts with about 450 members. The Mennonite Church Conference congregations total 150, and the Independent Mennonite Conference congregations also total about 150 baptized members.

Greenwood is the major Mennonite community in the state, with several congregations. The Old Order Amish settlement is to the west of Dover, with a Conservative Mennonite congregation in the capital city. There is also a Spanish-speaking congregation of the Lancaster Conference in Wilmington.

In the 1920s the public school officials made it very difficult for children and their parents of our faith because they refused to salute the flag. Today there is a network of our parochial elementary schools, a middle and high school in the state.

28. Idaho

There are five subgroups in Idaho, with thirteen congregations, and a total of about 1,200 Anabaptist-Mennonite followers.

The Church of God in Christ, Mennonites have over 530 members. The Dual Conference of the Pacific Northwest Mennonite Conference has 490 members. The Unaffiliated Mennonite Church congregation has about fifty members, and an Independent Mennonite Conference congregation at Cataldo has thirty-seven members. The Anabaptist Christian Fellowship at Grangeville is the smallest with twenty-six members.

There is both a large and small congregation next to the Canadian border at Bonners Ferry and Naples. There are several congregations in the southwest corner of the state at Boise, Nampa, and New Plymouth. And across the southern counties Anabaptist-

Mennonite communities can be found at Aberdeen, Buhl, Filer, Hammett, and Hazelton.

29. Georgia

The state of Georgia has about 1,150 members in nine Anabaptist-Mennonite subgroups with twenty-two congregations and fellowships.

The Beachy Amish Mennonite and Church of God in Christ, Mennonite groups each have about 280 members. The Dual Conference congregation in Atlanta counts about twenty members.

The Atlanta area, known as the hub of the south, has several congregations. Montezuma is a clustered community, with Americus nearby where Anabaptist-Mennonite constituents are located. To the southwest area are Colquitt, Cuthbert, and Meigs, and to the southeast, Jesup and Metter. From the center of the state to the east are the Dublin, Hephzibah, Stapleton, and Waynesboro communities, and to the northeast are Bowersville and Hartwell.

30. North Carolina

There are almost 1,100 members of the Anabaptist-Mennonite faith family in twenty-seven congregations, districts, and fellowships, in seven subgroups across North Carolina.

The largest group is the Mennonite Church Conference congregations with about 450 members, with Hickory as their center. Next are the Afro-American congregations of the Mennonite Brethren with 200 members, and Lenoir is their center. The smallest group is the Unaffiliated Mennonite congregations with fifty members, at Etowah and Tryon, in the southwest corner of the state.

The major cities where congregations are now located are Asheville, Durham, Greensboro, Rocky Mount, and Winston Salem. Within the last year the Charlotte fellowship closed because of a lack of leadership, one of the numerous casualties in our historical files.

The New Order Amish have established settlements in Union Grove and Yanceyville. The conservative and plain groups are in the rural eastern areas of Grifton, Pantego, and Severn, and across the state in Rutherfordton.

31. Montana

The Anabaptist-Mennonite membership across the Big Sky Country adds up to over 850 members in nineteen congregations, districts, and fellowships, among nine subgroups.

The largest group is the General Conference Mennonite congregations with about 240 members. In second place there are two groups: the Mennonite Brethren and Mennonite Church Conference congregations, each with about 170 members. The smallest group is the new Anabaptist Christian Fellowship at Roundup.

There are three Native Northern Cheyenne congregations in the southeast sector of the state. There are two Old Order Amish districts involved in logging in the northwest corner. Cities where congregations are found are Glendive, Kalispell, and Wolf Point. Smaller towns with congregations nearby are Bloomfield, Coalridge, Corvallis, Fairfield, and Lustre.

32. Alabama

This Deep South state has four subgroups, sixteen congregations, and a total of over 800 Anabaptist-Mennonites.

The major city of Birmingham has three congregations and fellowships, and the gulf coastal city of Mobile has one. A decade ago there was a bi-racial church planting effort in the capital city of Montgomery which failed.

The main rural center is in the southern sector at Atmore and Brewton. A large prison ministry is based at Atmore. To the far north the communities of Hartselle, Locust Fork, and Springville each have a congregation. In the west central sector groups are located at Amelle, Faunsdale, and Orrville. Several Afro and Native American fellowships are active in the state.

The largest group is the Mennonite Church Conference with about 450 members. Then, the Church of God in Christ, Mennonite communities with about 280 members. Next are the Beachy Amish Mennonites with over fifty members, and an Unaffiliated Mennonite congregation with about fifty members.

33. Arkansas

The Anabaptist-Mennonite faith family in the state of Arkansas can count about 750 members, with seventeen congregations, districts, and fellowships in eleven subgroups.

The largest groups are the Amish Mennonites and the Church of God in Christ, Mennonites, each with about 200 members. The smallest is the Conservative Unaffiliated Happy Hollow congregation at Mountain View with thirteen members. This community has two other small congregations.

Communities are scattered in and near the small cities of Dumas, El Dorado, Harrison, Mena, and Rogers, and in the towns of Calico Rock, Gentry, Marshall, and Nashville. At one time there were fellowships in Conway and Little Rock.

34. Puerto Rico

The island of Puerto Rico, a territory of the States in the Caribbean, now has eighteen congregations with 680 members.

Two subgroups, the Mennonite Church Conference (Convention in Spanish) has 530 members in eleven congregations, and the Mennonite Church Independent Conferences have over 150 members in seven congregations.

In 1945 churches sprung up around Aibonito and La Plata following the witness of a Civilian Public Service unit, begun in 1943, and MCC VS. Congregations are now located in the major cities of Ponce and San Juan. The smaller cities of Bayamon and Caguas have congregations, along with the towns of Anasco, Arecibo, Barranquitas, Cayey, and Coamo, and several scattered in rural communities.

There is a large Mennonite hospital at Aibonito, serving the population in the center of the island.

35. North Dakota

The state of North Dakota numbers about 650 baptized members in twelve congregations in seven subgroups.

The largest group is the Mennonite Brethren with 250 members, and their Central District Office is located at Bismarck. Next is an Independent Mennonite congregation at Munich with over ninety members, and the smallest group is a General Conference congregation at Alsen with twenty-seven members.

Congregations are scattered from Fargo to Minot, and in between communities can be found at Casselton, Grafton, Harvey, Mylo, and Wolford.

Because of the economic tides against small- to medium-sized farming operations in the Midwest, many of our people have taken flight from the prairie communities.

36. Louisiana

There are two groups of Anabaptist-Mennonites in the Bayou State with six congregations and 600 members.

The Mennonite Church Gulf States Conference has a Spanish-speaking congregation in a suburb of New Orleans, one in the Cajun French community of Des Allemands, and at the fishing village of Venice. A new Native Christian outreach has opened at Gretna.

The Church of God in Christ, Mennonites have a large community in the southwest corner of the state at De Ridder and a smaller one in the northeast Delta country at Transylvania.

37. South Carolina

In South Carolina there are four subgroups, ten congregations, and 590 members in the Anabaptist-Mennonite faith family.

The largest group is the Beachy Amish congregations with 210 members; then the Unaffiliated Mennonite congregations with about 190 members. Next is the Independent Conference congregation at Barnwell with over eighty members, followed by the Mennonite Church Conference congregations with about sixty members.

The various Mennonite communities are mainly settled along the western side of the state. There are congregations in the cities of Anderson and Charleston. Columbia, the capital city, at one time had an active fellowship, but the leader was called to an overseas assignment and the group folded.

Abbeville is a center, with other communities such as Blackville, Cross Hill, Fair Play, Honea Path, New Holland, and Pickens hosting congregations.

38. New Jersey

The Mennonite Church Conferences have thirteen congregations with a membership of 587 up and down the state of New Jersey. There is one Independent Conference congregation with thirty-six members at Vineland. There are three Hispanic congregations, one also at Vineland, and one each in the cities of Camden and Trenton. There are several bi-racial congregations active in the state, and a couple fellowships are located in the Camden south suburbs. The fellowship at Cardiff endeavors to reach into Atlantic City.

Allow me to move from reporting and ask a couple questions: from the strong Anabaptist-Mennonite base in southeastern Pennsylvania, why do we have so little outreach, and so few converts in nearby New Jersey? Why are we not located in any of the thickly-populated northeast Jersey cities and suburbs?

---

39. West Virginia

The Mountain State has five subgroups of Anabaptist-Mennonites with sixteen congregations and 552 members.

The Mennonite Church Conference congregations have 220 members, as the largest group, and the smallest is the Mennonite Christian Fellowship at Gap Mills with over fifty.

About ten congregations are an extension into the eastern hill country from the strong Anabaptist-Mennonite base in the Shenandoah Valley of Virginia. Morgantown is the only city in the state with a congregation, which is Church of the Brethren/Mennonite. Towns where congregations are established include Bunker Hill, Harman, Mathias, Phillipi, and Seneca Rocks.

40. New Mexico

This state can count 428 baptized members in twelve congregations and fellowships in seven subgroups.

The Mennonite Fellowship churches with about ninety members is the largest group. The Conservative Mennonite Conference with nearly eighty members is second, and the smallest group is the Beachy Amish settlement at Mimbres in the southwest corner of the state.

Half of the congregations are clustered in Albuquerque and suburbs. Two congregations are in the northwest corner of the state at Farmington. At Bloomfield there is a Brethren in Christ mission to the Navajo Nation. Belen and Carlsbad each have a congregation.

41. District of Columbia

The Nation's Capital has five congregations and fellowships in two subgroups, Mennonite Church and Unaffiliated Mennonite, with a total of 322 members. There is an Afro-American congregation on Peabody Street which belongs to the Lancaster Conference, and Conquest Fellowship belongs to the Virginia Conference. Washington Community is a growing congregation near Capital Hill. The other two are Community House and Fellowship Haven.

42. Massachusetts

There are two groups in the state, with four congregations and 273 members. Three Lancaster Mennonite Conference congregations serve basically two ethnic groups, the Anglos and Chinese. There is a Dual Conference congregation with about fifty members. All are located in the suburbs of Boston. The Mennonites finally reached out to New England about forty years ago.

43. Connecticut

The Lancaster Conference has three Mennonite congregations in three cities. Bridgeport has a Hispanic congregation, Hartford has a Laotian congregation, and New Haven has an Afro-American congregation. There is a total of 202 baptized members across Connecticut.

44. Vermont

There are three groups of Anabaptist-Mennonites in the state of Vermont, with five congregations and 200 members. There are also three Franconia Conference congregations, an unaffiliated congregation, and one Independent Conference congregation. The towns in or near where those churches can be found are Andover, Bridgewater Corners, Essex Junction, Taftsville, and Wolcott.

45. Maine

The state of Maine has four subgroups of Anabaptist-Mennonites, in five congregations and fellowships, but only ninety-eight adult members. The Lancaster Conference has congregations in the cities of Augusta and Portland. The Beachy Amish have a fellowship at Albion, the Old Order Mennonite Unaffiliated community is located at Oakfield, and the Church of God in Christ, Mennonites have a new mission at Bridgewater.

46. Hawaii

For a number of years there has been Anabaptist-Mennonite church planting efforts on the Isles in a cooperative program of Franconia and Lancaster Mennonite Conferences. In the major city of Honolulu there are both a Hawaiian Anglo and a Vietnamese congregation with a total of seventy-eight members.

47. Wyoming

Since 1991 there has been one congregation at Carpenter east of Cheyenne. There are seventeen members in this High Prairie congregation of the Mennonite Fellowship Churches.

48. Alaska

The Prince of Peace Mennonite congregation at Anchorage has a membership of nine persons. There was a fellowship active some years ago, but it was later discontinued. A recent expansion is a Mennonite Voluntary Service Unit.

49. Utah

Between the writing and the release of this book, the Mennonite Fellowship Churches have commissioned a minister and deacon with their families to relocate to Garland, in northern Utah, to establish a new Fellowship, the first in that state.

50. Nevada, New Hampshire, and Rhode Island

These are the three states where there is no current Anabaptist-Mennonite presence or witness. However, in each of these states there has been activity in the past.

A decade or more ago there was a Mennonite Church Fellowship forming in Reno, Nevada. But upon one of the early visits of a firm oversight person who sensed openness on sexuality issues, the group was disbanded. Some decades ago there was a Mennonite Voluntary Service Unit in one of the public institutions in New Hampshire for several years. And during World War II there were two Mennonite Civilian Public Service Units stationed in Rhode Island.

Observations

We are called at times "The Quiet in the Land." As a religious minority we are now speaking out more often for others who are suffering from oppression, and are powerless and voiceless.

As of June 30, 1997, we can count forty-six groups of Anabaptist-Mennonites across the span of the States, a total of 3,474 congregations, districts, and fellowships, with a grand total of 302,256 baptized members.

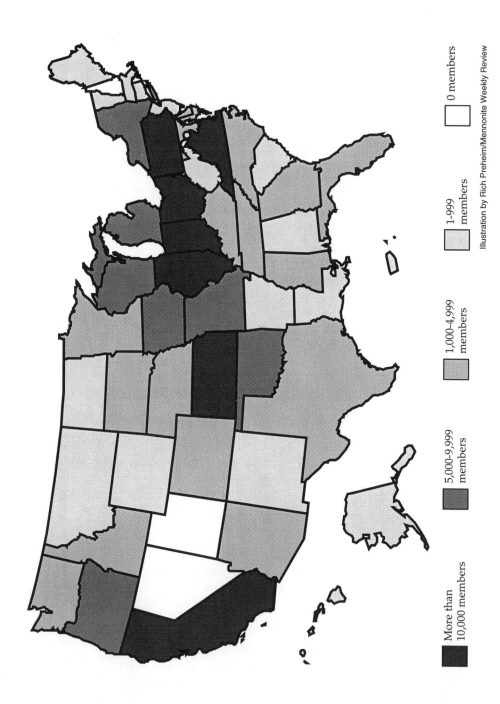

Illustration by Rich Preheim/Mennonite Weekly Review

More than
10,000 members

5,000-9,999
members

1,000-4,999
members

1-999
members

0 members

Alabama

		Congregations	Members
Mennonite Church Conference			
Atmore	Christian Fellowship		
Atmore	Oak Drive		
Atmore	Poarch Community		
Birmingham	Family of God		
Birmingham	New Life Harvest		
Birmingham	South Side		
Brewton	Bethel		
Brewton	Calvary		
Locust Fork	Faith Chapel		
Mobile	Mobile		
Springville	Straight Mountain	11	453
Church of God in Christ, Mennonite			
Emelle	Southern Star		
Faunsdale	Cedar Crest	2	284
Beachy Amish Mennonite			
Hartselle	Emmanuel		
Orrville	Orrville	2	54
Mennonite Church, Unaffiliated			
Atmore	Gospel Light	1	47
*(4)**	*Alabama Total*	*16*	*838*

Alaska

		Congregation	Members
Mennonite Church Conference, Northwest			
Anchorage	Prince of Peace	1	9

Arizona

		Congregations	Members
Dual Conference (Pacific Southwest GC/MC)			
Chandler	Koinonia		
Chinle	Black Mountain		

---

*The number of sub-groups for each state appear in italics and in parenthesis in the lower left of each state listing.

Glendale	Trinity		
Phoenix	First		
Phoenix	Good Shepherd		
Phoenix	Inter-Tribal		
Phoenix	Sunnyslope		
Prescott	Prescott		
Surprise	Emmanuel		
Tucson	Shalom	10	986
Church of God in Christ, Mennonite			
Chambers	Klagetoh/Wide Ruins		
El Mirage	Sun Valley		
Greasewood	Greasewood		
Keams Canyon	Jeddito		
Willcox	Mountain Valley	5	145
Conservative Mennonite Conference			
Paradise Valley	Paradise Valley		
Phoenix	Crossroads		
Phoenix	Dios Con Nosotros		
Phoenix	Grace		
Phoenix	SW Navajo	5	141
Mennonite Church Independent Conference			
Chinle	Blue Gap		
Wickenburg	Berea	2	62
Mennonite Brethren			
Phoenix	Desert Valley	1	41
Independent Mennonite			
Hotevilla	Gospel		
Kykotsmovi	Oraibi	2	38
Mennonite Church, Unaffiliated			
Chinle	Upper Room		
Cottonwood	Waterless Mesa	2	24
American Baptist/Mennonite			
Hotevilla	Bacavi	<u>1</u>	<u>6</u>
(8)	*Arizona Total*	*28*	*1,443*

Arkansas

		Congregations	Members
Amish Mennonite			
Green Forest	Green Forest		
Mena	Mount Zion		
Nashville	Mineral Springs	3	208

Church of God in Christ, Mennonite

Dumas	Three Rivers		
Gentry	Gentry	2	207

Mennonite Church Conference

Calico Rock	Bethel Springs		
Calico Rock	Calico Rock	2	74

Mennonite Brethren

Marshall	Martin Box		
Siloam Springs	Grace	2	62

Beachy Amish Mennonite

Harrison	Hillcrest		
Mountain View	Shady Lawn	2	61

Mennonite Church, Unaffiliated

Mountain View	West Richwoods	1	35

Conservative Mennonite Conference

Eldorado	First	1	31

Church of the Brethren/Mennonite

Rogers	Brethren/Mennonite	1	21

Mennonite Church Independent Conference

Strawberry	Strawberry	1	18

Old Order Amish

Lincoln	Lincoln	1	15

Conservative Mennonite, Unaffiliated

Mountain View	Happy Hollow	1	13

(11)	*Arkansas Total*	*17*	*745*

California

		Congregations	*Members*
Mennonite Brethren			
Dinuba	Dinuba		
Downey	Living Hope		
Fresno	Bethany		
Fresno	Butler Avenue		
Fresno	Faith		
Fresno	Fig Garden		
Fresno	North		
Kingsburg	Kingsburg		
Lodi	Vinewood		
Reedley	Reedley		
San Jose	Lincoln Glen		
Shafter	Shafter	12	4,118

Mennonite Brethren Bible

Bakersfield	Heritage		
Bakersfield	Laurelglen		
Bakersfield	Rosedale		
Coarsegold	Mountain		
Los Angeles	City Terrace		
Madera	Madera Avenue		
Orland	Country		
San Jose	Blossom Valley		
Santa Clara	El Camino	9	1,997

Mennonite Brethren Hispanic

Arleta	Cristo es la Repuesta		
Bakersfield	Aposento Alta		
Bakersfield	Vida Nueva		
Dinuba	Templo Calvario		
Madera	Templo Getsemani		
North Hollywood	Iglesia de Restauracion		
Orange Cove	El Buen Pastor		
Orosi	Templo La Paz		
Parlier	Hermanos Menonitas		
Raisin City	Iglesia de Comunidad		
Reedley	El Faro		
San Jose	Iglesia de los Hechos		
Shafter	Evangelica Encuentro		
Traver	Templo de Oracion	14	654

Mennonite Brethren Neighborhood

Sacramento	Greenhaven		
Visalia	Visalia	2	483

Mennonite Brethren Community

Capitola	Grace		
Clovis	College		
Clovis	Mountainview		
Eldorado Hills	Village		
Fresno	West Park		
Roseville	Oaks	6	436

Mennonite Brethren Slavic/Ukranian

Fresno	Slavic Evangelical		
Sacramento	First Ukranian		
San Leandro	Slavic	3	373

Mennonite Brethren Asian

Anaheim	Bethany Korean		
Bonita	Japanese Bible		
Fresno	Butler Avenue KHMU		
Fresno	North Fresno Japanese		
Los Angeles	Cho Dai Church		
Los Angeles	Korean Agape		

Los Angeles	Korean Missionary		
Los Angeles	Na Sung Ban Suk		
Santa Clara	India Community		
Upland	Grace Chinese	10	249

Mennonite Brethren African-American

San Jose	Ethiopian	1	92

Mennonite Brethren Fellowship

Union City	New Life	1	21
	Total	58	8,423

Dual Conference (Pacific Southwest GC/MC)

Arroyo Grande	Servant Community		
Buena Park	Trinity Taiwanese		
Chino Hills	Indonesian Hosana		
Claremont	Peace Fellowship		
Cupertino	Cupertino		
Downey	Faith		
Downey	Indonesian Imanuel		
Fresno	Community		
Fresno	Hmong Church of God		
Fresno	Hmong Community		
Fullerton	Indonesian Sion		
Inglewood	Calvary		
La Mirada	Indonesian Sion		
La Puente	House of the Lord		
Los Angeles	Family I		
Los Angeles	Family II		
Los Angeles	Iglesia Monte Sinai		
Los Angeles	Prince of Peace		
North Hollywood	Evangelica Bethel		
Orange	Indonesian Bethel		
Pasadena	Pasadena		
Pasa Robles	First		
Reedley	First		
Reedley	Vida Nueva		
Reseda	Indonesian Maranatha		
San Diego	Fellowship		
San Francisco	Chinese		
San Francisco	First		
Santa Fe Springs	Bethel		
Sierra Madre	Indonesian Anugrah		
Upland	First		
Upland	Fuente de Vida		
Upland	Mountain View	32	2,102

Brethren in Christ

Alta Loma	Alta Loma		
Alta Loma	Lord's House		
Chino	Chino		
Etiwanda	Etiwanda		
Moreno Valley	Community		
Ontario	Christo La Roca		
Ontario	Ontario		
Pomona	New Community		
Riverside	Agua Viva		
Riverside	Riverside		
Upland	Upland		
Valinda	Getsemani		
Walnut	Walnut Valley	13	1,499

Church of God in Christ, Mennonite

Anaheim	Mission		
Glenn	Glenn		
Livingston	Livingston		
Winton	Winton	4	773

Mennonite Fellowship Churches

Alturas	Alturas		
Fortuna	North Coast	2	48

Mennonite Christian Fellowship

Beckwourth	Sierra Valley	1	4
(5)	*California Grand Total*	*110*	*12,869*

Colorado

		Congregations	Members
Mennonite Church Rocky Mountain Conference			
Cheraw	East Holbrook		
Colorado Springs	Beth El		
Colorado Springs	First		
Denver	First		
Glenwood Springs	Glenwood Springs		
Grand Junction	Community		
Greeley	Greeley		
Julesburg	Julesburg		
La Junta	Emmanuel		
Lakewood	Glennon Heights		
Limon	Limon		
Pueblo	Pueblo		

Rocky Ford	Rocky Ford		
Walsenburg	Walsenburg	14	1,149
Dual Conference (GC/MC)			
Aurora	Peace		
Fort Collins	Fort Collins		
Palmer Lake	Mountain Community	3	214
Mennonite Brethren			
Denver	Garden Park		
Denver	Korean Mustard Seed		
Littleton	Bellevue Acres	3	186
General Conference Mennonite			
Arvada	Arvada		
Boulder	Boulder		
Vona	New Friedensburg	3	115
Church of God in Christ, Mennonite			
Center	High Valley		
Fort Garland	Valley		
Montrose	Mesa View	3	98
Mennonite/Presbyterian			
LaJara	United	1	48
Mennonite Church Independent Conference			
Montrose	Sunny View	1	35
Mennonite Fellowship Church			
Loma	Grand Valley	1	22
Brethren in Christ			
Colorado Springs	Oakwood Community	1	19
Anabaptist Christian Fellowship			
Bellvue	Hope	1	18
(10)	*Colorado Total*	*31*	*1,904*

Connecticut

		Congregations	Members
Mennonite Church, Lancaster Conference			
Bridgeport	Gospel Light		
Hartford	Laotian		
New Haven	Bible Fellowship	3	202

Delaware

		Congregations	Members
Conservative Mennonite Conference			
Bridgeville	Cannon		
Dover	Central		
Greenwood	Greenwood		
Greenwood	Laws	4	602
Old Order Amish District			
Dover	East		
Dover	Lower North		
Dover	Middle North		
Dover	South		
Dover	Upper North		
Hartly	Middle South		
Hartly	West		
Wyoming	Southeast	8	440
Mennonite Church Conference			
Greenwood	Tressler		
Wilmington	Centro de Amor	2	154
Mennonite Church, Independent Conference			
Bear	Highland		
Delmar	Pine Shore		
Kenton	Kenton	3	148
(4)	*Delaware Total*	17	1,344

District of Columbia

	Congregations	Members
Mennonite Church Conference		
Conquest Fellowship		
Peabody Street		
Washington Community	3	278
Mennonite Church, Unaffiliated		
Community House		
Fellowship Haven	2	44
(2) *District of Columbia Total*	5	322

Florida

		Congregations	Members

Mennonite Church, Southeast Conference

Apopka	Iglesia Ebenezer
Arcadia	Pine Creek
Blountstown	Oak Terrace
Cape Coral	Cape Christian
Coral Gables	Amor Viviente
Fort Myers	Arca de Salvacion
Gainesville	Emmanuel
Homestead	Homestead
Immokolee	Immokolee
Laurel	Worship Center
Miami	Good Shepherd
Miami	Nouveau Testament
Miami	Tabernacle of Bethlehem
North Port	Peace
Opa-Locka	New Hope
Saint Petersburg	Saint Petersburg
Sarasota	Ashton
Sarasota	Bahia Vista
Sarasota	Bay Shore
Sarasota	Newtown Gospel
Sarasota	Seguidores de Cristo
Tampa	College Hill
Tampa	North Tampa

Mennonite Church, Lancaster Conference

Century	Byrneville		
Crestview	Crestview		
Jay	Cobbtown	26	2,460

Brethren in Christ

Hialeah	Cristo Vive
Hialeah	Ebenezer
Hialeah	Hermanos in Cristo
Hialeah	Maranatha
Hialeah	Nueva Jerusalem
Homestead	Homestead
Kendall	Bethel
Miami	Cristo Rey
Miami	Fuente de Salvacion
Miami	Genesis
Miami	Monte Calvario
Orlando	Holden Park
Palm Harbor	East Lake

		Congregations	Members
Pembroke Pines	Aposanto de la Gracia		
Sarasota	Community Bible	15	1,017
Conservative Mennonite Conference			
Blountstown	Bethel		
Florida City	Southmost		
Sarasota	Bethel		
Sarasota	Cross Haven		
Sarasota	Friendship		
Sarasota	Palm Grove		
Tallahassee	Berean		
Tavares	Trinity	8	666
Church of God in Christ, Mennonite			
Sarasota	Gospel Center		
Walnut Hill	Walnut Hill	2	206
Mennonite Church, Unaffiliated			
Blountstown	Red Oak		
Bushnell	Grace		
Sarasota	Sarasota		
Sarasota	Tourist	4	192
Beachy Amish Mennonite			
Dade City	Pleasantview		
Sarasota	Sunnyside	2	172
Old Order Amish			
Sarasota	Pinecraft	1	93
Mennonite Church Independent Conference			
Arcadia	Peace River		
Pensacola	Pensacola	2	41
Dual Conference (GC/MC)			
Miami	Encuentro de Renovacion	1	40
(9)	*Florida Total*	*61*	*4,887*

Georgia

		Congregations	Members
Church of God in Christ, Mennonite			
Bowersville	North Georgia		
Edgehill	Harmony Springs		
Stapleton	Pinecrest	3	291
Beachy Amish Mennonite			
Jesup	Lake Grace		
Montezuma	Clearview		
Montezuma	Montezuma	3	280

Mennonite Church Independent Conference

Dublin	Dublin		
Hephzibah	Hephzibah		
Metter	Metter		
Waynesboro	Burkeland	4	176

Mennonite Church, Unaffiliated

Colquitt	Colquitt		
Hartwell	Hartwell		
Meigs	Meigs		
Montezuma	Gospel Light		
Wrightsville	Glad Tidings	5	160

Mennonite Church Conference

Americus	Americus		
Atlanta	Berea		
Decatur	Cell-ebration	3	98

Brethren in Christ

Lawrenceville	Grace	1	69

Conservative Mennonite Conference

Cuthbert	Faith	1	36

Anabaptist Christian Fellowship

Dublin	Emmanuel	1	21

Dual Conference (GC/MC)

Atlanta	Atlanta	1	17

(9)	*Georgia Total*	22	*1,148*

Hawaii

		Congregations	Members
Mennonite Church Conferences, Franconia and Lancaster			
Honolulu	New Life		
Honolulu	Vietnamese	2	78

Idaho

		Congregations	Members
Church of God in Christ, Mennonite			
Bonners Ferry	Mountain View		
Buhl	Buhl		
Filer	Valley View		

Hazelton	Canyon		
New Plymouth	Treasure Valley	5	560

Dual Conference (Pacific Northwest GC/MC)

Aberdeen	First		
Boise	Hyde Park		
Filer	Filer		
Nampa	First	4	491

Mennonite Church, Unaffiliated

Hammett	Indian Cove		
Naples	Kootenai Valley	2	80

Mennonite Church, Independent Conference

Cataldo	Cataldo	1	37

Anabaptist Christian Fellowship

Grangeville	Jubilee	1	26
(5)	*Idaho Total*	*13*	*1,194*

Illinois

	Congregations	Members

Mennonite Church Conference

Arthur	Arthur
Cazenovia	Cazenovia
Chicago	Bethel
Chicago	Englewood
Chicago	Ethiopian Evangelical
Chicago	Iglesia Cristiano
Chicago	Iglesia Gethsemani
Chicago	Lawndale
Chicago	Metro Ministries
Chicago	Reba Place-Rogers Park
Cicero	Centro Cristiano
Cicero	Sonido de Albanza
East Peoria	East Peoria
East Peoria	Pleasant Hill
Eureka	Living Praise
Eureka	Maple Lawn
Fisher	East Bend
Flanagan	Waldo
Freeport	Freeport
Henry	Trinity New Life
Hopedale	Hopedale
Kankakee	People for Reconciliation
Lombard	Lombard

Metamora	Metamora		
Moline	Templo Albanza		
Morton	First		
Morton	Trinity		
Peoria	First Norwood		
Peoria	Living Love		
Roanoke	Roanoke		
Saint Anne	Rehoboth		
Sterling	Science Ridge		
Summit Argo	Iglesia Peniel		
Tiskilwa	Willow Springs		
Tremont	Dillon	35	3,691

General Conference Mennonite

Carlock	Carlock		
Chicago	Comunidad de Fe		
Chicago	First		
Chicago	Grace Community		
Congerville	Congerville		
Danvers	North Danvers		
Flanagan	Flanagan		
Hopedale	Boynton		
Meadows	Meadows		
Pekin	Bethel		
Washington	Calvary	11	1,589

Old Order Amish Districts

Arcola	Bagdad
Arcola	East Chesterville
Arcola	North Cook Mills
Arcola	South Bourbon
Arcola	West Prairie
Arthur	Cadwell
Arthur	County Line
Arthur	East Prairie
Arthur	Lake Fork
Arthur	North Cadwell
Arthur	North Fairbanks
Arthur	Northeast Fairbanks
Arthur	North Prairie
Arthur	Southeast Fairbanks
Arthur	Southwest Fairbanks
Arthur	South Prairie
Arthur	Tri-County
Arthur	West Chesterville
Colchester	McDonough
Flat Rock	Crawford
Humboldt	Cooks Mill

Mount Vernon	Mount Vernon		
Opdyke	Opdyke		
Pleasant Hill	Pike		
Sullivan	Jonothan Creek		
Sullivan	Jonothan Creek II		
Tuscola	North Bourbon	27	1,485

Evangelical Mennonite Church

Dewey	Dewey		
East Peoria	Oak Grove		
Eureka	Bible		
Gridley	Salem		
Groveland	Groveland		
Morton	Grace		
Normal	Heartland		
Palos Hills	Calvary Memorial		
Peoria	Northwoods	9	1,282

Dual Conference (GC/MC)

Champaign-Urbana	First		
Evanston	Evanston		
Markham	Community		
Mundelein	North Suburban		
Normal	Normal		
Oak Park	Oak Park		
Peoria	Joy Fellowship		
Peoria	Peoria North		
Peoria	United		
Schaumburg	Christ Community		
Tiskilwa	Plow Creek	11	698

Amish Mennonite

Roanoke	Linn		
Roanoke	North Linn		
Shelbyville	Mount Herman		
Tampico	Fairfield	4	342

Beachy Amish Mennonite

Arcola	Pleasant View		
Arthur	Trinity		
Carrier Mills	Carrier Mills		
Clayton	Siloam Springs	4	287

Mennonite Church of the Brethren

Evanston	Reba Place	1	264

Conservative Mennonite Conference

Arthur	North Vine		
Arthur	Sunnyside	2	236

Mennonite Church, Independent Conference

Anna	Mount Pleasant		

Ewing	Ewing		
Keenes	Orchardville	3	178
Mennonite Church, Unaffiliated			
Freeport	Shalom		
Wayne City	Sunnyside	2	67
Reformed Mennonite			
Sterling	Sterling	1	43
Brethren in Christ			
Morrison	Morrison	1	32
New Order Amish			
Ava	Shawnee	1	21
Church of God in Christ, Mennonite			
Arthur	Prairie	1	13
Mennonite Brethren			
Chicago	Lakeview	1	11
(16)	*Illinois Total*	*114*	*10,239*

Indiana

		Congregations	Members
Old Order Amish Districts			
Berne	East		
Berne	Middle East		
Berne	North Middle		
Berne	Northeast Berne		
Berne	Northwest Berne		
Berne	South Middle		
Berne	West Berne A		
Berne	West Berne B		
Bourbon	South Millwood		
Bremen	East Bremen		
Bremen	North Hepton		
Bremen	South Hepton		
Bremen	West Beech		
Bremen	West Burlington		
Bryant	South Wabash		
Bryant	Southwest		
Canaan	East		
Canaan	West		
Economy	Economy		
Etna Green	Community Center		
Etna Green	Community Center North		

Geneva	East
Geneva	East Jefferson
Geneva	North Wabash
Geneva	South
Geneva	Southeast
Geneva	Southeast District II
Geneva	South Jefferson
Geneva	South Wabash Valley
Geneva	Southwest
Geneva	West
Goshen	Clinton Center
Goshen	Clinton Prairie
Goshen	East Clinton
Goshen	Fish Lake
Goshen	Middle Forks
Goshen	North Clinton
Goshen	Southwest Clinton
Goshen	West Clinton
Goshen	West Honeyville
Goshen	West Middle Clinton
Grabill	Middle West
Grabill	Northeast
Grabill	Northeast II
Grabill	Northwest
Grabill	Northwest II
Greensburg	South Flatrock
Hamilton	Steuben
Hamilton	Steuben West
Howe	Middle West
Howe	Northeast
Howe	Northeast II
Lagrange	Bloomfield
Lagrange	Clearspring 12
Lagrange	Clearspring 12-1
Lagrange	East Bloomfield
Lagrange	East Clearspring
Lagrange	Hawpatch
Lagrange	Lagrange
Lagrange	Northwest Lagrange
Lagrange	South Lagrange
Lagrange	Southeast Lagrange
Lagrange	Southwest Lagrange
Lagrange	Taylor
Lagrange	West Lagrange
Liberty	Liberty
Ligonier	East Noble

Ligonier	North Wauka
Ligonier	Wauka
Loogootee	Middle East
Loogootee	Northeaast
Loogootee	Southeast
Marshall	Marshall
Middlebury	Forks
Middlebury	Middle Barrens 53
Middlebury	Middle Barrens 54
Middlebury	Middle Clinton
Middlebury	North Barrens
Middlebury	North Clinton
Middlebury	North Forks
Middlebury	Northeast Clinton
Middlebury	Northwest Barrens
Middlebury	Northwest Barrens-70
Middlebury	Northwest Barrens-70-1
Middlebury	Northwest Forks
Middlebury	South Forks
Middlebury	South Middle Barrens
Middlebury	West Barrens
Middlebury	West Forks
Milford	Hastings
Milford	Milford
Milford	Southeast
Milford	South Milford
Millersburg	East Millersburg
Millersburg	Middle West Honeyville
Millersburg	Millersburg
Millersburg	North Millersburg
Millersburg	Southeast Clinton
Millersburg	Southwest Honeyville
Milroy	Flat Rock
Milroy	Milroy Middle
Monroe	Blue Creek
Monroe	North
Monroe	Northeast
Monroe	Northeast Monroe
Monroe	Northwest Monroe
Monroe	Southwest Monroe
Monroe	West Blue Creek
Montgomery	East
Montgomery	Middle East
Montgomery	Middle East Center
Montgomery	Middle East Northeast
Montgomery	Middle Northwest

Montgomery	Middle South
Montgomery	Montgomery
Montgomery	Southwest
Montgomery	West
Nappanee	East Millwood
Nappanee	Hepton
Nappanee	Locke
Nappanee	Nappanee
Nappanee	North
Nappanee	North Beech Road
Nappanee	North Millwood
Nappanee	Northwest
Nappanee	South Nappanee
Nappanee	Southwest
Nappanee	Tri-County
Nappanee	Union Center
Nappanee	Union Center East
Nappanee	Weldy
Nappanee	West Burkholder
Nappanee	West Nappanee
Nappanee	West Union Center
New Haven	Northeast
New Haven	North Southwest
New Haven	Southeast
New Haven	Southwest
Odon	Middle North
Odon	Northeast
Odon	Northwest
Odon	Prairie Creek
Orleans	Orleans
Rockville	Bellmore
Rushville	East
Salem	East Washington
Salem	Salem
Shipshewana	East Forks
Shipshewana	East Shipshewana
Shipshewana	East Yoder Corner
Shipshewana	Middle Shipshewana 44
Shipshewana	Middle Shipshewana 45
Shipshewana	North Forks
Shipshewana	North Shipshewana
Shipshewana	North Middle Shipshewana
Shipshewana	Northeast Barrens
Shipshewana	Northeast Barrens None
Shipshewana	Northeast Shipshewana
Shipshewana	Northside District 50

Shipshewana	Northside District 50-1		
Shipshewana	North Yoder Corner		
Shipshewana	Ship Lake		
Shipshewana	Shipshewana 42		
Shipshewana	Shipshewana 44-1		
Shipshewana	South Middle Shipshewana		
Shipshewana	South Shipshewana 41		
Shipshewana	South Shipshewana 41-2		
Shipshewana	Southeast Barrens		
Shipshewana	Southeast Yoder Corner		
Shipshewana	West Shipshewana		
Shipshewana	Yoder Corner		
South Whitley	South Whitley		
Spencerville	East Spencerville I		
Spencerville	East Spencerville II		
Spencerville	West Spencerville		
Topeka	East Honeyville		
Topeka	Eden		
Topeka	Honeyville		
Topeka	Middle Topeka		
Topeka	North Honeyville		
Topeka	Northeast Clearspring		
Topeka	Northeast Emma		
Topeka	Northeast Topeka		
Topeka	South Honeyville		
Topeka	Southeast Clearspring		
Topeka	Southeast Emma		
Topeka	Southeast Topeka		
Topeka	Southwest Topeka		
Topeka	Topeka		
Topeka	West Clearspring		
Topeka	West Noble		
Topeka	West Topeka		
Vevay	Pleasant		
Wolcottville	East Johnson		
Wolcottville	North Wolcottville		
Wolcottville	Wolcottville	204	11,170

Mennonite Church Conference

Bean Blossom	Bean Blossom
Benton	Benton
Bloomington	Fellowship
Bristol	Bonneyville
Bristol	Tri-Lakes
Cannelburg	Berea
Elkhart	Belmont
Elkhart	Church Without Walls

Elkhart	Fellowship of Hope
Elkhart	House of Power
Elkhart	Olive
Elkhart	Prairie Street
Elkhart	Roselawn
Elkhart	Sunnyside
Fort Wayne	Anderson
Fort Wayne	Central
Fort Wayne	Fairhaven
Fort Wayne	First
Goshen	Berkey Avenue
Goshen	Clinton Brick
Goshen	Clinton Frame
Goshen	College
Goshen	del Buen Pastor
Goshen	East Goshen
Goshen	Faith
Goshen	Gospel Lighthouse
Goshen	North Goshen
Goshen	Pleasant View
Goshen	Walnut Hill
Goshen	Waterford
Goshen	Yellow Creek
Howe	Marion
Hudson Lake	Hudson Lake
Indianapolis	First
Indianapolis	Shalom
Kokomo	Howard-Miami
Kokomo	Parkview
Kouts	Hopewell
Lagrange	Plato
Leo	North Leo
Middlebury	First
Middlebury	Forks
Montgomery	First
Mongomery	Providence
Nappanee	Maranatha
Nappanee	North Main Street
Odon	Bethel
Rensselaer	Burr Oak
Shipshewana	Shore
South Bend	Kern Road
South Bend	Restoration
Stroh	Lake Bethel
Syracuse	Wawasee Lakeside
Topeka	Emma

Valparaiso	Valparaiso		
Wakarusa	Holdeman		
Warsaw	Warsaw	57	9,714

General Conference Mennonite

Berne	First		
Elkhart	Hively Avenue		
Fort Wayne	Maplewood		
Goshen	Eighth Street		
Goshen	Silverwood		
Middlebury	Pleasant Oaks		
Nappanee	First		
Topeka	Topeka	8	2,208

Conservative Mennonite Conference

Austin	Austin		
Goshen	Maple City Chapel		
Goshen	Mount Joy		
Goshen	Pine Ridge		
Goshen	Pleasant Grove		
Harlan	Sunrise		
Middlebury	Griner		
Shipshewana	Roselawn		
Shipshewana	Townline	9	1,107

Evangelical Mennonite Church

Angola	Sonlight		
Berne	Evangelical		
Fort Wayne	Brookside		
Fort Wayne	Highland Bethel		
Fort Wayne	Pine Hills		
Grabill	Evangelical		
Upland	Evangelical		
Woodburn	Westwood	8	1,093

Mennonite Church, Unaffiliated

Bourbon	New Vine		
Butlerville	Butlerville		
Evansville	Believers Fellowship		
Kokomo	Rich Valley		
Kouts	Cornerstone		
Loogootee	Believers		
Madison	Fellowship		
Martinsville	Martinsville		
Milford	Milford Chapel		
Nappanee	South Union		
New Haven	Good Shepherd		
New Paris	Salem		
North Judson	English Lake		
North Judson	Toto		

Topeka	Eden		
Topeka	Maple Grove		
Walkerton	Fish Lake	17	1,049

Beachy Amish Mennonite

Berne	Fellowship		
Bourbon	Clay Street		
Bremen	Berea		
Goshen	Fair Haven		
Goshen	Woodlawn		
Kokomo	Bethany		
Lagrange	Hebron		
Millersburg	Southhaven		
Montgomery	Mount Olive		
Nappanee	Maple Lawn		
New Haven	Ridgeview		
Woodburn	Fellowship Haven	12	882

Old Order Mennonite, Wisler Conference

Goshen	Yellow Creek		
Mentone	Southside		
Nappanee	Fairview	3	385

Mennonite Church, Independent Conference

Canaan	Canaan		
Goshen	Grace		
Millersburg	Bethany		
Nappanee	Bethel Conservative		
Nappanee	Sandy Ridge		
North Liberty	North Liberty		
Washington	Fresh Start	7	375

Dual Conference (GC/MC)

Elkhart	Southside		
Goshen	Assembly		
Lafayette	Fellowship		
Muncie	Morning Star		
Paoli	Paoli	5	359

Old Order Mennonite, Indiana Groffdale Conference

Goshen	Yellow Creek		
Nappanee	Blossers		
Tippecanoe	Tippecanoe		
Wakarusa	Clearland	4	350

Brethren in Christ

Garrett	Christian Union		
Marengo	Mount Zion		
Nappanee	Nappanee		
New Paris	Union Grove	4	242

Conservative Mennonite, Unaffiliated

Grabill	Cuba

Montgomery	Pleasant View		
Raglesville	Mount Joy	3	239
New Order Amish			
Kokomo	North		
Kokomo	South		
Salem	Salem		
Worthington	Worthington	4	195
Mennonite Church and Church of the Brethren			
Goshen	Communion	1	102
Anabaptist Christian Fellowship			
Goshen	Victory	1	72
Old Order Mennonite, Weaver Group			
Goshen	Yellow Creek	1	45
Amish Mennonite, Unaffiliated			
Nappanee	Fairview	1	34
Church of God in Christ, Mennonite			
Hardinsburg	Southern Hills	1	19
Dual Conference Mennonite/Church of Brethren			
South Bend	Emanuel	1	14
(20)	*Indiana Total*	*351*	*29,654*

Iowa

		Congregations	Members
Mennonite Church Conference			
Burlington	Peace		
Davenport	Iglesia Emanuel		
Des Moines	Des Moines		
Fort Dodge	Evangelical		
Iowa City	First		
Kalona	East Union		
Kalona	Kalona		
Kalona	Lower Deer Creek		
Manson	Manson		
Mount Pleasant	Pleasant View		
Muscataine	Muscataine		
Parnell	West Union		
Washington	Washington		
Wayland	Bethel		
Wayland	Sugar Creek		
Wellman	Daytonville		
Wellman	Wellman	17	2,848

Old Order Amish Districts

Bloomfield	Middle		
Bloomfield	North		
Bloomfield	South		
Bloomfield	West		
Chariton	Chariton		
Cresco	Cresco		
Drakesville	North West		
Edgewood	Edgewood		
Fairbank	Northwest		
Fairbank	South Central		
Fairbank	Southwest		
Hazleton	East Middle		
Hazleton	Northeast		
Hazleton	Southeast		
Kalona	Kalona Community		
Kalona	Middle		
Kalona	Middleburg		
Kalona	Middle East		
Kalona	Middle North		
Kalona	Northeast		
Kalona	Northwest		
Kalona	Pleasant Valley		
Kalona	Southwest		
Maquoketa	Jackson		
Milton	Middle		
Milton	North		
Milton	South		
Redding	Redding		
Riceville	Riceville North		
Riceville	Riceville South		
Seymour	Seymour	31	1,705

General Conference Mennonite

Ames	Ames		
Donnellson	Zion		
Pulaski	Pulaski		
Wayland	Eicher Emmanuel		
Wayland	Wayland	5	527

Conservative Mennonite Conference

Kalona	Fairview		
Kalona	Sunnyside		
Leon	Mount Zion		
New Boston	New Boston		
Wellman	Upper Deer Creek	5	433

Beachy Amish Mennonite

Kalona	Sharon Bethel		

Leon	Leon Salem	2	172
Church of God in Christ, Mennonite			
Bloomfield	Bloomfield		
McIntire	Heartland		
Lime Springs	Lime Springs	3	138
Old Order Mennonite, Groffdale Conference			
Charles City	Cedar Valley		
Riceville	Riceville	2	95
Mennonite Fellowship Church			
Kalona	Haven	1	50
Mennonite Church, Unaffiliated			
Kalona	Bethany		
Keota	Salem	2	49
Brethren in Christ			
Des Moines	Oak Park	1	37
Old Order River Brethren			
Dallas Center	Iowa District	1	34
Dual Conference (GC/MC)			
Cedar Falls	Cedar Falls	1	32
Anabaptist Christian Fellowship			
Wellman	Zion	1	22
Old Order Mennonite, Weaverland Conference			
Osage	Nora Springs	1	18
(14)	*Iowa Total*	*73*	*6,160*

Kansas

		Congregations	*Members*
General Conference Mennonite			
Buhler	Buhler		
Buhler	Hebron		
Burrton	Burrton		
Durham	Central Heights		
Elbing	Zion		
Goessel	Alexanderwohl		
Goessel	Goessel		
Halstead	First		
Hanston	Hanston		
Hillsboro	First		
Hillsboro	Trinity		
Hutchinson	First		
Inman	Bethel		
Inman	Hoffnungsau		

Inman	Inman		
Kingman	Kingman		
Liberal	Calvary		
McPherson	First		
Moundridge	Eden		
Moundridge	First Christian		
Moundridge	Hopefield		
Moundridge	West Zion		
Newton	Faith		
Newton	First		
Newton	New Creation		
Newton	Tabor		
North Newton	Bethel College		
Pawnee Rock	Bergthal		
Pretty Prairie	First		
Ransom	First		
Salina	Salina		
Whitewater	Grace Hill		
Wichita	Hope		
Wichita	Lorraine Avenue	35	8,937

Church of God in Christ, Mennonite

Burns	Eden		
Cimarron	Cimarron		
Copeland	Salem		
Dodge City	Dodge City		
Durham	Morning Star		
Fredonia	Emmanuel		
Galva	Lone Tree		
Galva	United Center		
Greensburg	Bethel		
Halstead	Garden View		
Halstead	Grace		
Hesston	Meridian		
Hillsboro	Alexanderfeld		
Ingalls	Living Hope		
Inman	Zion		
Lakin	Lakin		
Montezuma	Homeland		
Montezuma	Montezuma		
Moundridge	Gospel		
Plains	Plains View		
Scott City	Scott		
Sharon Springs	Sharon Springs		
Ulysses	Grant	23	3,553

Mennonite Brethren

Buhler	Buhler		

Cimarron	Valleyview		
Garden City	Garden Valley		
Hays	North Oak		
Hesston	Hesston		
Hillsboro	Ebenfeld		
Hillsboro	Hillsboro		
Hillsboro	Parkview		
Inman	Zoar		
Marion	Good News		
Newton	Koerner Heights		
Olathe	Community Bible		
Topeka	Topeka		
Ulysses	Ulysses		
Wichita	First	15	3,521

Mennonite Church Conference

Canton	Spring Valley		
Greensburg	Greensburg		
Harper	Crystal Springs		
Harper	Pleasant Valley		
Hesston	Hesston		
Kansas City	Argentine		
Protection	Protection		
South Hutchinson	Faith		
South Hutchinson	South Hutchinson		
Yoder	Yoder	10	1,716

Independent Mennonite

Burns	First		
Hesston	Garden		
Meade	Emmanuel		
Whitewater	Emmaus		
Whitewater	Swiss	5	1,081

Dual Conference (GC/MC)

Hesston	Inter-Mennonite		
Hesston	Whitestone		
Kansas City	Rainbow		
Lawrence	Peace		
Lenexa	New Hope		
Montezuma	Faith		
Newton	Shalom		
North Newton	Jubilee		
Topeka	Southern Hills		
Wichita	Church of the Servant	10	1,050

Old Order Amish District

Garnett	North		
Garnett	South		
Haven	Middle		

Haven	North		
Haven	South		
Hutchinson	West	6	330
Brethren in Christ			
Abilene	Abilene		
Abilene	Zion		
Hope	Rosebank	3	310
Evangelical Mennonite Church			
Hutchinson	Cornerstone		
Newton	Grace		
Sterling	Sterling	3	309
Beachy Amish Mennonite			
Hutchinson	Cedar Crest		
Hutchinson	Center	2	289
Conservative Mennonite Conference			
Hutchinson	Maranatha		
Hutchinson	Plainview	2	178
Evangelical Mennonite Brethren			
Meade	Meade	1	140
New Order Amish District			
Hutchinson	Amish	1	80
Tri-Conference (GC/MB/MC)			
Manhatten	Manhatten	1	60
Mennonite Evangelical Church			
Montezuma	Evangelical	1	16
(15)	*Kansas Total*	*117*	*21,570*

Kentucky

		Congregations	Members
Old Order Amish Districts			
Crab Orchard	Crab Orchard		
Dunnville	East		
Dunnville	West		
Glasgow	East		
Glasgow	West		
Gradyville	North		
Gradyville	South East		
Gradyville	South West		
Hardyville	Three Springs		
Hopkinsville	Hopkinsville		
Horse Cave	Waterloo Valley		
Hustonville	Huston		

Marion	Marion North		
Marion	Marion South		
Marion	Marion West		
Merrimac	Taylor		
Munfordville	Cub Run		
Munfordville	Cub Run East		
Munfordville	Logsden Valley		
Pembroke	Pembroke		
Sonora	Sonora		
Springfield	Springfield	22	1,210

Beachy Amish Mennonite

Auburn	Plainview		
Casey Creek	Casey		
Franklin	Franklin		
Franklin	Providence		
Hickory	Hickory		
Leitchfield	Cedar Springs		
Monticello	Pleasant Ridge	7	420

New Order Amish

Crofton	Crofton		
Guthrie	North		
Guthrie	Penchem		
Guthrie	South	4	240

Brethren in Christ

Campbellsville	Campbellsville		
Columbia	Beulah Chapel		
Columbia	Bloomington Chapel		
Columbia	Millersfield		
Knifley	Knifley		
Wilmore	Blue Grass	6	232

Old Order Mennonite, Groffdale Conference

Liberty	Cedar Hill		
Pembroke	Meadow Valley	2	210

Conservative Mennonite Conference

Altro	Bowlings Creek		
Clayhole	Caney Creek		
Lexington	Lexington		
Louisville	Louisville		
Oneida	Panco		
Rowdy	Buckhorn Creek		
Talbert	Turners Creek	7	194

Mennonite Fellowship Churches

Crockett	Faith Hills		
Flat Gap	Hope Valley		
Leburn	Valley View		
Sample	Breckenridge	4	180

Old Order Mennonite, Noah Hoover Group

| Scottsville | Oak Grove | | |
| Scottsville | Red Hill | 2 | 160 |

Old Order Amish, Swartzentruber Group

Park City	Park City East		
Park City	Park City West		
Upton	Swartzentruber	3	149

Church of God in Christ, Mennonite

| Murray | Harmony | 1 | 145 |

Mennonite Christian Fellowship

| Wallingford | Mount Carmel | 1 | 80 |

Amish Mennonite, Unaffiliated

| Mount Herman | Monroe County | 1 | 78 |

Mennonite Church Conference

Morgantown	Ridgeview		
Talcum	Talcum		
West Liberty	West Liberty	3	62

Old Order Mennonite, Unaffiliated

Ghent	Carroll County		
Hestand	Hestand		
Holland	Christian Community	3	61

Mennonite Church, Independent Conference

| Manchester | Pace's Creek | 1 | 29 |

Old Order Mennonite, Stauffer Group

| Elk Horn | Stauffer | 1 | 23 |

Reidenbach Old Order Mennonite

| Fairview | Hoover | 1 | 22 |

Dual Conference (GC/MC)

| Harlan | Harlan | 1 | 16 |

Mennonite Church, Unaffiliated

| Manchester | Wild Cat | 1 | 12 |

| *(19)* | *Kentucky Total* | 72 | 3,523 |

Louisiana

		Congregations	Members

Mennonite Church Conference

Buras	Lighthouse		
Des Allemands	Des Allemands		
Gretna	Native Christian		
Metaire	Amor Viviente	4	327

Church of God in Christ, Mennonite

| DeRidder | Highland | | |

Transylvania	Delta	_2_	_282_
(2)	*Louisiana Total*	6	609

Maine

		Congregations	Members
Mennonite Church, Lancaster Conference			
Augusta	Kennebec		
Portland	Church of the Servant	2	72
Beachy Amish Mennonite			
Albion	Plain	1	13
Old Order Mennonite, Unaffiliated			
Oakfield	Christian Community	1	10
Church of God in Christ, Mennonite			
Bridgewater	Maple Grove	_1_	_3_
(4)	*Maine Total*	5	98

Maryland

		Congregations	Members
Mennonite Church, Lancaster Conference			
Baltimore	Wilkens Avenue		
Baltimore	Evangelical Ethiopian		
Columbia	First		
Conowingo	Oakwood		
Dawsonville	Dawsonville		
Gaithersburg	Gaithersburg		
Hagerstown	Community		
Hagerstown	Mount Zion		
Jessup	Guilford Road		
Laurel	Capital Christian		
Laurel	New Life		
Laytonsville	Goshen		
Mount Airy	Mount Airy		
Sharpsburg	Dargan	14	525
Mennonite Church, Allegheny Conference			
Accident	Glade		
Grantsville	Oak Grove		
Pinto	Pinto		

Swanton	Meadow Mountain	4	373

Mennonite Church, Atlantic Coast Conference

Baltimore	North Baltimore		
Hagerstown	Hebron		
Hagerstown	North Side		
Ocean City	Ocean City		
Westover	Holly Grove	5	324

Mennonite Church, Virginia Conference

Hyattsville	Iglesia Completo	1	125

Mennonite Church, Franklin Conference

Westminster	Lighthouse	1	20
	Total	25	1,367

Mennonite Church, Independent Conference (Washington)

Cearfoss	Reiffs		
Clear Spring	Clear Spring		
Flintstone	Flintstone		
Hagerstown	Paradise		
Keedysville	Meadow View		
Leitersburg	Millers		
Smithsburg	Pondsville		
Smithsburg	Stouffers		
Williamsport	Pinesburg	9	1,010

Mennonite Church Independent Conference (Cumberland Valley)

Brownsville	Yarrowsburg		
Clear Spring	Lanes Run		
Maugansville	Mount Olive	3	156

Mennonite Church, Independent Conference (Eastern Pennsylvania)

Mechanicsville	Mechanicsville		
Mount Airy	Hopewell	2	85

Mennonite Church, Independent Conference (Bethel Conservative)

Salisbury	Salisbury	1	43
	Total	15	1,294

Old Order Amish District

Charlotte Hall	New Market		
Charlotte Hall	North		
Mechanicsville	East		
Mechanicsville	Middle		
Mechanicsville	Ryceville	5	405

Conservative Mennonite Conference

Accident	Cherry Glade		
Grantsville	Maple Glen		
Snow Hill	Snow Hill	3	390

Brethren in Christ

Essex	Faith		
Hagerstown	Paramount		
Walkersville	Walkersville		
Williamsport	Van Lear	4	231

New Order Amish

Oakland	Oakland	1	183

Dual Conference (GC/MC)

Hyattsville	Hyattsville	1	124

Old Order Mennonite, Stauffer Group

Loveville	Loveville	1	120

Mennonite Church, Unaffiliated

Grantsville	Red Run		
Swanton	Dry Run	2	108

Beachy Amish Mennonite

Cumberland	Friendship Haven		
Millington	Harmony	2	97

Mennonite Christian Fellowship

Swanton	Swanton	1	71

Mennonite Fellowship Church

Hagerstown	Hagerstown	1	62

Church of the Brethren/Mennonite

Oakland	Gortner Union	1	10

(13)	*Maryland Grand Total*	62	4,462

Massachusetts

		Congregations	Members
Mennonite Church, Lancaster Conference			
Boston	Chinese Saving Grace		
Malden	Malden		
Needham	Good Shepherd	3	221
Dual Conference (GC/MC)			
Somerville	Boston	1	52
(2)	*Massachusetts Total*	4	273

Michigan

Old Order Amish Districts

Blanchard	Blanchard
Bronson	Bronson-Orland
Burr Oak	South Middle
Camden	Camden South
Camden	Graber
Camden	Graber East
Cass City	Cass City
Centreville	Northeast 73
Centreville	Northeast 73-Z
Centreville	North Middle
Centreville	Southeast
Centreville	Southwest
Centreville	South Middle
Charlotte	North
Charlotte	South
Charlotte	Southwest
Clare	Clare East
Clare	Clare Northwest
Clare	Clare West
Coral	Coral
Gladwin	Gladwin
Gladwin	North
Gladwin	South
Greenville	Greenville
Greenville	Greenville North
Hale	Hale
Hillsdale	Hillsdale
Holton	Holton
Homer	Homer
Ludington	East Ludington
Ludington	West Ludington
Manton	Manton
Marion	Osceola
Marlette	Marlette
Marlette	Marlette II
Mio	Oscoda East
Mio	Oscoda West
Montgomery	California South
Montgomery	Southwest
Newaygo	Newaygo
Ossineke	Alpena
Ovid	Elsie

Quincy	North		
Quincy	South		
Reading	California North		
Reading	Reading		
Sears	Osceola		
Stanwood	Stanwood		
Stanwood	Stanwood Northeast		
Stanwood	Stanwood West		
Sturgis	Northwest		
Vestaburg	Vestaburg	52	2,860

Mennonite Church Conference

Ashley	Bethel		
Battle Creek	Pine Grove		
Brimley	Wayside		
Brutus	Maple River		
Burr Oak	Locust Grove		
Centreville	Wasepi		
Clarklake	Liberty		
Colon	South Colon		
Detroit	Peace Community		
Engadine	Wildwood		
Escanaba	Soo Hill		
Fairview	Fairview		
Germfask	Germfask		
Grand Marias	Grand Marias		
Gulliver	Maple Grove		
Harbor Springs	Stutzmanville Chapel		
Imley City	Bethany		
Lake Odessa	West Odessa		
Mancelona	Coldsprings		
Manistique	Cedar Grove		
Midland	Midland		
Naubinway	Naubinway		
Petoskey	Hilltop		
Menominee	Menominee River		
Pigeon	Michigan Avenue		
Pinckney	Good News		
Rexton	Rexton		
Saginaw	Grace Chapel		
Saginaw	Ninth Street		
Sturgis	Christian Fellowship Center		
Three Rivers	Moorepark		
Waldron	Salem	32	2,218

Conservative Mennonite Conference

Clarksville	Bowne		
Dowagiac	North Wayne		

Flint	Grace		
Mount Morris	Mount Morris		
National City	National City		
Pigeon	Pigeon River		
Sebewaing	Fairhaven		
Turner	Riverside		
Vassar	Pine View		
White Pigeon	Riverview	10	655

Church of God in Christ, Mennonite

Carson City	Mount Calm		
Ithaca	Newark	2	377

Evangelical Mennonite Church

Adrian	Good Shepherd		
Grand Blanc	Community		
Lawton	Evangelical		
Midland	Our Redeemer	4	236

Mennonite Church, Unaffiliated

Brethren	Pleasantview		
Carson City	Fellowship		
Hillsdale	Faith		
Sturgis	Calvary Chapel		
White Cloud	White Cloud	5	229

Brethren in Christ

Cassopolis	Bethel Community		
Leonard	Leonard		
Merrill	Bethel		
Owosso	Carland-Zion		
Sandusky	Mooretown		
Goodrich	Lakeview	6	211

Dual Conference (GC/MC)

Ann Arbor	Ann Arbor		
Detroit	Community		
Detroit	Fellowship		
East Lansing	MSU Fellowship	4	131

Mennonite Church, Independent Conference

Charlevoix	Grace Fellowship		
Constantine	Shiloh		
Mio	Conservative Fellowship		
Pelkie	Pelkie		
Seney	Seney		
Traverse City	Traverse Bay	6	102

General Conference Mennonite

Comins	Comins	1	97

Old Order Mennonite, Wisler Conference

Snover	Bethany	1	80

Beachy Amish Mennonite
Nottawa	Pilgrim	1	42

New Order Amish
Rosebush	Rosebush	1	40

Dual Conference (Mennonite/Church of the Brethren)
Ann Arbor	Shalom	1	30

Old Order Mennonite, Groffdale Conference
Sheridan	Vickeryville	1	30

Reformed Mennonite
Shelby	Shelby	1	30

Mennonite Fellowship Church
Fairview	Fairview Conservative	1	14

Old Order Mennonite, Unaffiliated
Le Roy	Cedar Road	1	8

(18)	*Michigan Total*	*130*	*7,420*

Minnesota

		Congregations	Members
General Conference Mennonite			
Butterfield	Butterfield		
Delft	Immanuel		
Duluth	Disciples		
Minneapolis	Hmong		
Mountain Lake	Bethel		
Mountain Lake	First		
Mountain Lake	Gospel		
Mountain Lake	Lao Christian		
Rochester	Fellowship		
Saint Paul	Saint Paul	10	1,121
Old Order Amish Districts			
Bertha	South		
Canton	Canton		
Canton	Northeast		
Canton	Southeast		
Granger	Granger		
Harmony	Harmony		
Long Prairie	Long Prairie		
Pine City	Pine City		
Preston	Northwest		

Utica	Utica		
Utica	Utica South		
Wadena	Wadena		
Wadena	Wadena South	13	715
Mennonite Brethren			
Brooklyn Park	Russian Evangelical		
Delft	Carson		
Mountain Lake	Mountain Lake		
New Hope	New Hope	4	592
Evangelical Mennonite Brethren			
Mountain Lake	Mountain Lake	1	180
Mennonite Church Conference			
Detroit Lakes	Lake Region		
International Falls	Point of Pines		
Jackson	Hilltop		
Leader	Leader		
Ogema	Strawberry Lake	5	171
Dual Conference (GC/MC)			
Minneapolis	Faith		
Roseville	Emmanuel	2	155
Conservative Mennonite Conference			
Blackduck	Kitchi Pines		
Bovey	Balsam Lake		
Nashwauk	Cloverdale	3	81
Mennonite Church Independent Conference			
Blooming Prairie	Prairie		
Littlefork	Northwood	2	76
Beachy Amish Mennonite			
Grove City	Believers	1	75
Church of God in Christ, Mennonite			
Kensington	Lake Haven	1	36
Mennonite Church, Unaffiliated			
Loman	Black River	1	25
(11)	*Minnesota Total*	*43*	*3,227*

Mississippi

		Congregations	Members
Church of God in Christ, Mennonite			
Brooksville	Brooksville		
Clarksdale	Clarksdale		
Egypt	Egypt		
Leland	Leland		

Macon	South Haven		
West Point	West Point	6	867

Mennonite Church Conference

Gulfport	Gulfhaven		
Jackson	Open Door		
Louisville	Choctaw Christian		
Macon	Cornerstone		
Meridian	Jubilee		
Philadelphia	Pearl River		
Preston	Nanih Waiya		
Quitman	Grace	8	398

Mennonite Church, Unaffiliated

Aberdeen	Mennonite Christian, North		
Aberdeen	Mennonite Christian, South		
Crawford	Faith		
Macon	Fellowship of Hope	4	175

Conservative Mennonite, Unaffiliated

Macon	Magnolia		
Macon	Oak Grove		
Taylorsville	Maranatha	3	126

Old Order Amish

Randolph	Pontotoc	1	30

Mennonite Church Independent Conference

Kokomo	Darbun	1	24
(6)	*Mississippi Total*	23	1,620

Missouri

		Congregations	*Members*

Old Order Amish Districts

Anabel	Anabel
Boonville	Prairie Home
Bowling Green	Northwest
Bowling Green	South
Bowling Green	Canton
Carrollton	Carrollton
Clark	Middle East
Clark	Middle West
Clark	Northeast
Clark	Northwest
Clark	Southeast
Clark	Southwest
Curryville	Northwest

Dixon	Dixon		
Humansville	Humansville		
Jamesport	East		
Jamesport	Middle		
Jamesport	North Clear		
Jamesport	Northwest		
Jamesport	South Clear		
Jamesport	West		
Kahoka	Kahoka		
La Plata	East La Plata		
La Plata	West La Plata		
Mount Vernon	Mount Vernon		
Raymondville	Raymond		
Milan	Milan		
Seymour	Seymour East		
Seymour	Seymour Middle East		
Seymour	Seymour North		
Seymour	Seymour Northeast		
Seymour	Seymour South		
Seymour	Seymour Southeast		
Verona	Verona North		
Verona	Verona South		
Wheatland	Wheatland		
Windsor	North Windsor		
Windsor	South Windsor	38	2,070

Mennonite Church Conference

Birch Tree	Berea		
Garden City	Sycamore Grove		
Hannibal	Cornerstone		
Harrisonville	Harrisonville		
Leonard	Mount Pisgah		
Palmyra	Pea Ridge		
Saint Louis	Bethesda		
Saint louis	Ethiopian Redeemer		
Versailles	Cornerstone		
Warsaw	Evening Shade	10	639

Amish Mennonite

Buffalo	Pleasant View		
Sedalia	Olive Hill		
Vandalia	Vandalia	3	535

Church of God in Christ, Mennonite

Jamesport	Jamesport		
Rich Hill	Bethany		
Versailles	Beulah		
Stover	Oak Ridge		
Walker	Living Faith	5	482

Old Order Mennonite, Weaverland Conference

Arbela	North View		
Latham	Pleasant Hill		
Memphis	Indian Creek		
Rutledge	Millport	4	479

Old Order Mennonite, Groffdale Conference

Garnett	Hopewell		
Latham	Clear View	2	425

Mennonite Church, Independent Conference

La Monte	La Monte		
Latham	Spring Hill		
Seymour	Ozark		
Summersville	Summersville		
Versailles	Versailles	5	321

Mennonite Christian Fellowship

Fairview	Fairview		
Lamar	Golden City		
LaRussell	Spring River	3	234

General Conference Mennonite

Fortuna	Bethel	1	195

Beachy Amish Mennonite

Linn	Mint Hill		
Linneus	Locust Creek		
Paris	Pleasant View	3	132

Dual Conference (GC/MC)

Saint Louis	Saint Louis	1	83

Old Order Mennonite, Stauffer Group

Tunas	Tunas	1	70

Mennonite Fellowship Church

Grandin	Grandin	1	51

Reidenbach Old Order Mennonite

Barnett	Reidenbach	1	36

Mennonite Church, Unaffiliated

Eldorado Springs	Rock Springs	1	30

Old Order Mennonite, Hoover Group

Rich Hill	Rich Hill	1	24

Mennonite/Church of Brethren

Columbia	Columbia	1	11

Mennonite Brethren

Lee's Summit	Summit	1	10

Old Oder Mennonite, John Martin Group

Barnett	House Church	1	8

(19)	*Missouri Total*	*83*	*5,835*

Montana

		Congregations	Members
General Conference Mennonite			
Ashland	Ashland		
Bloomfield	Bethlehem		
Busby	White River Cheyenne		
Lame Deer	Lame Deer		
Wolf Point	Bethel	5	237
Mennonite Brethren			
Lustre	Lustre		
Wolf Point	Gospel	2	168
Mennonite Church Conference			
Bloomfield	Red Top		
Coalridge	Coalridge		
Kalispell	Mountain View	3	164
Evangelical Mennonite Brethren			
Lustre	Lustre	1	91
Old Order Amish Districts			
Libby	Libby		
Rexford	Rexford	2	85
Mennonite Church, Unaffiliated			
Rexford	Kootenai		
Valley View	Rocky Mountain	2	40
Mennonite Church Independent Conference			
Corvallis	Woodside		
Fairfield	Fairfield	2	37
Dual Conference (GC/MC)			
Glendive	White Chapel	1	27
Anabaptist Christian Fellowship			
Roundup	Roundup	<u>1</u>	<u>10</u>
(9)	*Montana Total*	*19*	*859*

Nebraska

		Congregations	Members
General Conference Mennonite			
Beatrice	Beatrice		
Beatrice	First		
Henderson	Bethesda	3	1,506
Mennonite Church Conference			
Beemer	Beemer		

		Congregations	Members
Broken Bow	First		
Milford	Bellwood		
Milford	Beth El		
Milford	East Fairview		
Milford	Milford		
Omaha	Northside		
Shickley	Salem		
Wood River	Wood River	9	1,219
Mennonite Brethren			
Grant	New Life		
Henderson	Henderson		
Omaha	Faith Bible		
Omaha	Iglesia Agua Viva		
Omaha	Millard	5	435
Church of God in Christ, Mennonite			
Friend	Mission		
Greeley	Cedar Hills		
Madrid	Golden Plains	3	209
Dual Conference (GC/MC)			
Lincoln	First		
Omaha	New Hope	2	79
Mennonite Church, Unaffiliated			
Beaver Crossing	West Fairview	<u>1</u>	<u>58</u>
(6)	*Nebraska Total*	*23*	*3,506*

New Jersey

		Congregations	Members
Mennonite Church Conference		*Congregations*	*Members*
Alpha	Alpha		
Camden	Manantial de Vida		
Cardiff	New Life		
Marlton	Crossroads Community		
Mizpah	Mizpah		
Norma	Norma		
Oxford	Grace		
Penns Grove	Friendship Chapel		
Stratford	Word Fellowship		
Trenton	Puerto de Sion		
Victory Gardens	Garden Chapel		
Vineland	City of Hope		
Vineland	Faro Ardiente	13	551

Mennonite Church, Independent Conference

Vineland	Vineland	1	36
(2)	*New Jersey Total*	*14*	*587*

New Mexico

		Congregations	Members
Mennonite Fellowship Churches			
Belen	Belen		
Farmington	Farmington	2	92
Conservative Mennonite Conference			
Albuquerque	Abundant Life		
Albuquerque	Living Word	2	82
Mennonite Church Conference			
Carlsbad	Carlsbad		
Farmington	Light of Life	2	78
Brethren in Christ			
Albuquerque	Sandia		
Bloomfield	Navajo Chapel	2	70
Dual Conference (GC/MC)			
Albuquerque	Albuquerque		
Rio Rancho	Family of Faith	2	61
Church of God in Christ, Mennonite			
Albuquerque	Mountain View	1	10
Beachy Amish Mennonite			
Mimbres	Mimbres Valley	1	13
(7)	*New Mexico Total*	*12*	*406*

New York

		Congregations	Members
Mennonite Church, New York Conference			
Addison	Jesus		
Akron	Clarence Center-Akron		
Alden	Alden		
Bath	Pleasant Valley		
Amsterdam	Bethel		
Buffalo	West Side		
Cattaraugus	Shalom		
Corning	Community		

East Syracuse	Syracuse		
Independence	Independence		
Lowville	Rhema		
New Bremen	First		
Rexville	West Union		
Rochester	Bethsaida Evangelical		
Watertown	Watertown		
Wellsville	York Corners		
Williamsville	Harris Hill		
Woodville	Woodville	18	1,179

Mennonite Church, Lancaster Conference

Bolivar	Kossuth		
Bronx	Evangelical Garifuna		
Bronx	King of Glory		
Bronx	North Bronx		
Brooklyn	Believers		
Brooklyn	Ebenezer Haitian		
Brooklyn	Evangelical Tabernacle		
Manhattan	Ethiopian Evangelical		
Manhattan	Seventh Avenue		
Queens	Iglesia Valle de Jesus		
Queens	Iglesia de Avivamiento		
Staten Island	Redeeming Grace	12	441

Mennonite Church, Atlantic Coast Conference

Bronx	Friendship Community		
Bronx	Iglesia Ebenezer		
Brooklyn	First		
Manhattan	Ephesians	4	130

Mennonite Church, Franconia Conference

Putnam Station	Log Chapel	1	25
	Total	36	1,775

Old Order Amish Districts

Addison	Addison
Cattaraugus	Axeville East
Cattaraugus	Axeville West
Clymer	West
Conewango Valley	Conewango East
Conewango Valley	Conewango West
Conewango Valley	Flat Iron
Conewango Valley	North
Conewango Valley	Northeast
Conewango Valley	Northwest
Conewango Valley	South
Conewango Valley	Southeast

Conewango Valley	West		
Fairfield	Newport		
Fillmore	Fillmore		
Fort Plain	East		
Fort Plain	West		
Friendship	Friendship		
Heuvelton	East		
Heuvelton	Middle		
Heuvelton	North		
Heuvelton	South		
Mayville	Mayville		
Norfolk	Norwood		
Panama	Southeast		
Prattsburg	Prattsburg		
Romulus	Fayette		
Romulus	Ovid		
Sherman	Northeast		
Woodhull	Woodhull North		
Woodhull	Woodhull South	31	1,705

Conservative Mennonite Conference

Brooklyn	Followers of Jesus		
Carthage	Carthage		
Castorland	Naumburg		
Croghan	Croghan		
Glenfield	Pine Grove		
Lowville	Lowville	6	1,050

Old Order Mennonite, Groffdale Conference

Dundee	Gravel Run		
Penn Yan	Benton		
Penn Yan	Milo		
Rushville	Rushville	4	655

Old Order Mennonite, Weaverland Conference

Fayette	Fayette		
South Butler	Pleasant Ridge	2	318

Mennonite Church Independent Conference

Belmont	Phillips Creek		
Croghan	Crystal Light		
Lakemont	Lakeland		
Waterloo	Waterloo	4	188

Dual Conference (GC/MC)

Brooklyn	Amor Viviente		
Manhattan	Manhattan		
Rochester	Rochester Area	3	169

Brethren in Christ

Bronx	Fellowship Chapel		
Clarence Center	Ransom Creek	2	135

Beachy Amish Mennonite
Dundee	Crystal Valley		
Henderson	Northern Light		
Perry	Silver Lake	3	115

Mennonite/Elim Fellowship
Flushing	Immanuel	1	109

Anabaptist Christian Fellowship
Bainbridge	Grace		
Philadelphia	Philadelphia	2	80

Mennonite Christian Fellowship
Madison	Madison	1	69

Mennonite Brethren
Rochester	First Ukranian		
Woodside	Bethania Telegu	2	36

Mennonite Fellowship Church
Lowville	Hope	1	27

Church of God in Christ, Mennonite
Auburn	Finger Lakes		
New York City	Mission	2	18

(15)	*New York Grand Total*	99	6,449

North Carolina

		Congregations	Members

Mennonite Church Conference
Asheville	Asheville		
Creston	Big Laurel		
Greensboro	Greensboro		
Hickory	Catawba Valley		
Hickory	Hickory		
Hickory	Mountain View		
Jefferson	Jefferson		
Lansing	Meadowview		
Rocky Mount	Fellowship of Christ		
Sanford	Bethel Christian		
Winston Salem	Oak Hill	11	440

Mennonite Brethren
Boone	Boone		
Ferguson	Darby		
Lenoir	Bushtown		
Lenoir	Laytown		
Lenoir	West End		
Newland	Beechbottom	6	205

Mennonite Fellowship Churches

Pantego	Hope		
Rutherfordton	Pine Ridge		
Severn	Severn	3	125

Dual Conference (GC/MC)

Durham	Durham		
Raleigh	Raleigh	2	99

Church of God in Christ, Mennonite

Grifton	Lighthouse	1	87

New Order Amish

Union Grove	Union Grove		
Yanceyville	Yanceyville	2	86

Mennonite Church, Unaffiliated

Etowah	United Covenant		
Tryon	Foothills	_2_	_46_

(7)	*North Carolina Total*	27	1,088

North Dakota

		Congregations	Members
Mennonite Brethren			
Bismarck	Washington Heights		
Harvey	Harvey		
McClusky	John's Lake		
Minot	Minot	4	254
Independent Mennonite			
Munich	Salem	1	93
Church of God in Christ, Mennonite			
Grafton	Grafton	1	90
Mennonite Church Conference			
Surrey	Fairview		
Wolford	Lakeview	2	84
Dual Conference (GC/MC)			
Casselton	Casselton		
Fargo	Fargo-Moorhead	2	63
Mennonite Church, Unaffiliated			
Mylo	Salem	1	35
General Conference Mennonite			
Alsen	Swiss	_1_	_27_
(7)	*North Dakota Total*	12	646

Ohio

	Congregations	Members

Old Order Amish Districts

Andover	Andover
Apple Creek	Apple Creek East
Apple Creek	Apple Creek Northeast
Apple Creek	Apple Creek Southeast
Apple Creek	Apple Creek Southwest
Apple Creek	Apple Creek West
Apple Creek	Maysville West
Ashland	East
Ashland	Middle
Ashland	Middle East
Ashland	Southeast
Ashland	Southwest
Baltic	Baltic
Baltic	Becks Mills
Baltic	Brush Run West
Baltic	Flat Ridge
Baltic	Flat Ridge East
Baltic	Flat Ridge South
Baltic	New Bedford East
Baltic	New Bedford North
Baltic	New Bedford Northeast
Baltic	New Bedford West
Barnesville	Barnesville
Beaver	Beaver
Bellville	Middle East
Bellville	Northeast
Bellville	Northwest
Bergholz	Bergholz
Berlin	Berlin
Berlin	Berlin Middle East
Berlin	Berlin Southeast
Bremen	Bremen
Burton	Burton
Burton	Troy Northeast
Burton	Troy Northwest
Burton	Troy South
Butler	North
Carrollton	Carroll
Charm	Charm East
Charm	Charm North
Charm	Charm Northeast
Charm	Charm Northwest

Charm	Charm South
Chesterhill	Chesterhill
Columbiana	Aldernick
Danville	Brinkhaven
DeGraff	DeGraff North
DeGraff	DeGraff South
Farmerstown	Farmerstown
Farmerstown	Farmerstown North
Farmerstown	Farmerstown Southeast
Farmerstown	Farmerstown Southwest
Farmerstown	Farmerstown South
Farmerstown	Farmerstown West
Fredericksburg	Elm Grove
Fredericktown	Middle West
Fredericktown	Southeast
Fredericktown	Southwest
Fredericktown	West
Fredericktown	West Waterford
Fresno	New Bedford Middle
Fresno	New Bedford South
Fresno	New Bedford Southwest
Gallipolis	Gallia
Garrettsville	Garrettsville
Garrettsville	Nelson
Greenwich	West
Hartville	King
Hicksville	Defiance County
Holmesville	Middle North
Holmesville	Middle West
Holmesville	North
Holmesville	North East
Holmesville	North West
Holmesville	Southeast
Holmesville	Southwest
Huntsburg	Huntsburg East
Huntsburg	Huntsburg Northeast
Huntsburg	Huntsburg Middle
Huntsburg	Huntsburg Southeast
Huntsburg	Huntsburg Southwest
Huntsburg	Huntsburg West
Huntsburg	Johnsons Corner NE
Jeromesville	Jeromesville
Kenton	Kenton Middle
Kenton	Kenton Northeast
Kenton	Kenton West
Kidron	Kidron

Kidron	Kidron South
Kinsman	Kinsman South
LaRue	Southeast
Martinsburg	Martinsburg I
Martinsburg	Martinsburg II
McKay	McKay
Mesopotamia	Mespo
Mesopotamia	Mespo Hill
Mesopotamia	Mespo Hill South
Mesopotamia	Mespo North
Mesopotamia	Mespo Northeast
Mesopotamia	Mespo Northwest
Mesopotamia	Mespo Southwest
Mesopotamia	Mespo West
Middlefield	Bundysburg Road NW
Middlefield	Burton Station
Middlefield	Burton-Windsor Road
Middlefield	Girdle Road
Middlefield	Girdle Road II
Middlefield	Hayes Corner
Middlefield	Hayes Corner East
Middlefield	Hayes Corner South
Middlefield	Hayes Corner West
Middlefield	Laird Road
Middlefield	Middlefield North
Middlefield	Middlefield Northeast
Middlefield	Middlefield North Middle
Middlefield	Middlefield Southeast
Middlefield	Middlefield West
Middlefield	Nauvoo
Middlefield	Newcomb Road
Middlefield	North Girdle Road
Middlefield	North Newcomb
Middlefield	Old State Road
Middlefield	South Burton
Middlefield	South Newcomb
Middlefield	Townline North 22B
Middlefield	Townline South
Middlefield	Windsor
Middlefield	Windsor II
Millersburg	Beechville Northeast
Millersburg	Beechville Southeast
Millersburg	Beechville West
Millersburg	Bunker Hill Middle
Millersburg	Bunker Hill North East
Millersburg	Bunker Hill North West

Millersburg	Bunker Hill South
Millersburg	Bunker Hill Southeast
Millersburg	Clark East
Millersburg	Clark West
Millersburg	Doughty East
Millersburg	Doughty West
Millersburg	Doughty Valley SE
Millersburg	Fairview East
Millersburg	Fairview West
Millersburg	Flat Ridge Northwest
Millersburg	Fryburg East
Millersburg	Fryburg West
Millersburg	Mill Creek
Millersburg	Sharp Run
Millersburg	Sharp Run East
Millersburg	Weaver Ridge
Mount Eaton	Mount Eaton
Mount Eaton	Mount Eaton North
Mount Eaton	Mount Eaton Southeast
Mount Eaton	Mount Eaton Southwest
Mount Hope	Mount Hope
Mount Hope	Mount Hope Middle East
Mount Hope	Mount Hope North
Mount Hope	Mount Hope Northwest
Mount Hope	Mount Hope South
Mount Hope	Mount Hope Southeast 61B
Mount Hope	Mount Hope Southeast 73B
Mount Hope	Mount Hope Southwest
Mount Hope	North Mount Hope
Orrville	East Union
Orrville	East Union East
Orrville	Northeast
Orwell	Bloomfield
Orwell	Orwell
Parkman	Frams Corner
Parkman	Parkman
Parkman	Parkman Middle
Parkman	Parkman North
Parkman	Parkman Northeast
Parkman	South
Parkman	Southeast
Patriot	Patriot
Pierpont	Pierpont
Plain City	Madison
Quaker City	Lewisville West
Salineville	Salineville

Salesville	Salesville		
Shiloh	Shiloh		
Shreve	Shreve South		
Somerset	Somerset		
Sugarcreek	Barrs Mills East		
Sugarcreek	Barrs Mills Northeast		
Sugarcreek	Barrs Mills Northwest		
Sugarcreek	Barrs Mills South		
Sugarcreek	Barrs Mills Southeast		
Sugarcreek	Barrs Mills Southwest		
Sugarcreek	Brush Run East		
Sugarcreek	East Troyer Valley		
Sugarcreek	Stoney Point		
Sugarcreek	Sugarcreek North		
Sugarcreek	Sugarcreek South		
Sugarcreek	West Troyer Valley		
Sugarcreek	West Union Valley		
Summerfield	Lewisville East		
Trail	Trail Northeast Annex		
Trail	Trail North		
Trail	Trail Southeast		
Trail	Trail West		
Walnut Creek	East Walnut Creek		
Walnut Creek	Walnut Creek North		
Walnut Creek	Walnut Creek Northeast		
Walnut Creek	Walnut Creek South		
Walnut Creek	Walnut Creek Upper		
Walnut Creek	Walnut Creek West		
West Farmington	Farmington East		
West Farmington	Farmington North		
West Farmington	Farmington Southeast		
West Farmington	Farmington West		
West Union	Wheat Ridge East		
Wilmot	East Valley		
Winchester	East Valley West		
Winesburg	Winesburg East		
Winesburg	Winesburg Middle		
Winesburg	Winesburg North 81		
Winesburg	Winesburg North 85		
Winesburg	Winesburg Northeast		
Winesburg	Winesburg Northwest		
Winesburg	Winesburg Southeast		
Winesburg	West 44		
Winesburg	West 47	228	12,493

Mennonite Church Conference

Archbold	Central

Archbold	Buen Pastor
Archbold	Zion
Aurora	Aurora
Barberton	Summit
Beaver	Owl Creek
Bellefontaine	Community
Berlin	Berlin
Burton	Pleasant Hill
Canton	Dayspring
Canton	First
Chesterville	Gilead
Cincinnati	Springdale Chapel
Cleveland	Friendship
Cleveland	Lee Heights
Cleveland	University Euclid
Cloverdale	Mount Pleasant
Columbiana	Midway
Dalton	Dove
Defiance	Primera Iglesia
Elida	Pike
Elida	Salem
Elyria	Peace
Fairpoint	Fairpoint
Fremont	Primera Iglesia
Hartville	Hartville
Jackson	Hillside
Kidron	Kidron
Kidron	Sonnenberg
Leetonia	Leetonia
Logan	Saint Johns
Louisville	Beech
Louisville	Stoner Heights
Millersburg	Gray Ridge
Millersburg	Martins Creek
Millersburg	Millersburg
Monclova	Emmanuel
New Carlisle	Huber
Newcomerstown	Flat Ridge
North Lawrence	Pleasant View
North Lima	North Lima
Orrville	Chestnut Ridge
Orrville	Martins
Orrville	Orrville
Pedro	Wayside Chapel
Pettisville	West Clinton
Plain City	Cornerstone

Plain City	Sharon		
Rittman	Crown Hill		
Shreve	Moorehead		
Smithville	Smithville		
Springfield	Northridge		
Springfield	Southside		
Stryker	Lockport		
Stryker	Pine Grove		
Toledo	Toledo		
Vinton	Fellowship Chapel		
Wadsworth	Bethel		
Walnut Creek	Walnut Creek		
Wauseon	Inlet		
Wauseon	North Clinton		
Wauseon	Tedrow		
West Lafayette	Lafayette		
West Liberty	Bethel		
West Liberty	Oak Grove		
West Liberty	South Union		
Winesburg	Longenecker		
Wooster	Salem		
Wooster	Wooster		
Youngstown	Berean	70	10,193

Conservative Mennonite Conference

Apple Creek	Fairlawn
Berlin	Grace
Berlin	Pleasant View
Burton	Maple View
Cincinnati	New Beginnings
Fredericksburg	Assembly
Hartville	Bethany
Hartville	Cornerstone
Hartville	Maple Grove
Hicksville	Hicksville
Hilliard	Agape
Irwin	Shiloh
Logan	Turkey Run
London	Shalom
Mechanicsburg	Mechanicsburg
Millersburg	United DaySpring
Mount Eaton	Calvary
Orrville	East Union
Plain City	Maranatha
Plain City	United Bethel
Shauck	Johnsville
Sugarcreek	Light in the Valley

West Salem	Fairhaven	23	3,320

General Conference Mennonite

Bluffton	First		
Kidron	Salem		
Pandora	Grace		
Pandora	Saint John		
Sugarcreek	First		
Trenton	Trenton		
Wadsworth	First	7	1,830

Old Order Amish, Ohio Dan Churches

Apple Creek	Maysville East		
Apple Creek	Maysville Northeast		
Apple Creek	Maysville Northwest		
Big Prairie	East Lakeville		
Danville	Danville		
Danville	Danville East		
Fredericksburg	Ashery East		
Fredericksburg	Ashery Northeast		
Fredericksburg	Ashery West		
Fredericksburg	Calmutier		
Fredericksburg	Calmutier North		
Fredericksburg	Calmutier Southwest		
Fredericksburg	Calmutier West		
Fredericksburg	Fredericksburg North		
Fredericksburg	Fredericksburg West		
Fredericksburg	Maysville Southwest		
Lakeville	Lakeville Middle East		
Lakeville	Lakeville Southeast		
Lakeville	West Lakeville		
Millersburg	Bunkerhill		
Millersburg	Bunkerhill East		
Millersburg	Bunkerhill Northeast		
Mount Hope	Mount Hope East		
Mount Hope	Mount Hope Northeast		
Mount Hope	Mount Hope Southeast		
Orrville	East		
Orrville	West		
Sugarcreek	Sugar Creek West	27	1,495

Beachy Amish Mennonite

Antrim	Antrim		
Bakersville	Salem		
Berlin	Bethel		
Fredericksburg	Shiloh		
Hartville	Pleasant View		
Holmesville	Peniel		
McConnelsville	Ebenezer		

Middlefield	Zion		
Millersburg	Fryburg		
Millersburg	Messiah		
Minerva	Minerva		
Pattersonville	Amana		
Plain City	Bethesda		
Plain City	Canaan		
Plain City	Haven		
Sugarcreek	Living Waters		
Sugarcreek	Maranatha		
Utica	Melita		
Winesburg	Grace Haven	19	1,426

Old Order Amish, Swartzentruber Group

Apple Creek	Fountain Nook		
Apple Creek	Maysville		
Apple Creek	Northwest		
Apple Creek	Stutzman and Troyer		
Dalton	West Lebanon		
Dalton	West Lebanon North		
Dundee	North		
Dundee	Southeast		
Dundee	South Middle		
Fredericksburg	Fountain Nook II		
Fredericksburg	Maysville West		
Fredericksburg	Salt Creek East		
Fredericksburg	Southwest		
Homerville	Homerville		
Homerville	Homerville Northwest		
Homerville	Middle West		
Kidron	Kidron		
Lodi	Lodi North Middle		
Millersburg	Becks Mills West		
Mount Eaton	Mount Eaton		
Peoli	Peoli		
Peoli	Peoli South		
Polk	Southwest		
Sullivan	West Middle		
West Salem	Southeast	25	1,375

Evangelical Mennonite Church

Archbold	Evangelical		
Perrysburg	Oak Bend		
Wauseon	Evangelical		
West Unity	Evangelical	4	1,346

New Order Amish

Belle Center	East		
Belle Center	Middle		

Belle Center	West		
Berlin	Berlin East		
Berlin	Berlin Northeast		
Fredericksburg	Elm Grove East		
Hartville	Amish		
Holmesville	West Holmesville		
Holmesville	Salt Creek West		
Kinsman	Kinsman		
Millersburg	East Martins Creek		
Millersburg	North Sharp Run		
Millersburg	West Martins Creek		
Leesburg	Highland County		
Mount Hope	Mount Hope		
Mount Hope	Mount Hope No. 2		
Sugarcreek	East Union Valley		
Sugarcreek	Sugarcreek East		
Sugarcreek	Cherry Ridge		
Walnut Creek	East Walnut Creek		
Walnut Creek	Lower Walnut Creek		
Walnut Creek	Walnut Creek Northwest		
Warsaw	Waldoning		
Winesburg	Winesburg	24	1,281

Brethren in Christ

Ashland	Ashland		
Cincinnati	Western Hills		
Dayton	Dayton		
Dayton	Mission		
East Canton	Valley Chapel		
Englewood	Fairview		
Massillon	Amherst		
Massillon	Sippo Valley		
New Carlisle	Gethsemane		
Pleasant Hill	Pleasant Hill		
Ravenna	Christ Chapel		
Springfield	Beulah Chapel		
Tipp City	Northgate		
West Milton	Highland		
Wooster	Wooster	15	936

Dual Conference (GC/MC)

Cincinnati	Fellowship		
Columbus	Agora Fellowship		
Columbus	Neil Avenue		
Dover	Dover		
Lima	Lima		
Smithville	Oak Grove		
West Liberty	Jubilee	7	808

Mennonite Church, Independent Conference

Carbon Hill	Carbon Hill		
Hartville	Hartville Conservative		
Leetonia	Mount Joy		
Maysville	Son Light		
Middlefield	Pilgrim		
Plain City	Deeper Life		
Trail	Gospel Light		
Wilmot	Country View	8	508

Mennonite Brethren

Parma	Slavic Missionary	1	505

Independent Mennonite

Bluffton	Ebenezer	1	490

Conservative Mennonite, Unaffiliated

Benton	Zion		
Hartville	Friendship		
Holmesville	Bethany		
Sugarcreek	Sharon	4	465

Mennonite Church, Unaffiliated

Andover	Crossroads		
Benton	Faith Haven		
Bladensburg	Mount Zion		
Elida	Sharon		
Millersburg	Gospel Haven		
North Lima	Christian Brethren	6	362

Old Order Mennonite, Ohio Wisler Group

Dalton	County Line		
Greenwich	Woodlawn		
Lisbon	Salem		
Wadsworth	Maple Hill	4	356

Old Order Amish, Tobe Hostetler Churches

Apple Creek	Hostetler East		
Apple Creek	Hostetler Middle East		
Apple Creek	Hostetler Middle West		
Fredericksburg	Hostetler West		
Wooster	Hostetler North	5	315

Church of God in Christ, Mennonite

Apple Creek	Rock of Ages		
Homeworth	Homeworth	2	257

Old Order Mennonite, Groffdale Conference

Shiloh	Blooming Grove		
Shiloh	Spring Mill	2	245

Old Order Mennonite, Wisler Conference

Columbiana	Pleasant View		
Wooster	Chester	2	208

Mennonite Fellowship Churches

Apple Creek	Bethel		
Columbiana	Sharon		
Kensington	Glade Run		
Patriot	Valley View		
Zanesville	Canaan	5	203

Anabaptist Christian Fellowship

Byesville	Cambridge		
Dalton	Calvary		
Martinsburg	Remnant		
Walnut Creek	Faith	4	157

Reformed Mennonite

Bluffton	Bluffton		
Marshallville	Marshallville		
Wauseon	Wauseon	3	70

Mennonite Christian Fellowship

Mount Perry	Calvary	1	57

Old Order Mennonite, Stauffer Group

Bainbridge	Bainbridge	1	18

(26)	*Ohio Total*	498	40,726

Oklahoma

	Congregations	*Members*
Mennonite Brethren		
Adams Adams		
Balko Balko		
Bethany Western Oaks		
Broken Arrow Slavic Missionary		
Collinsville Westport		
Cordell Bible		
Corn Corn		
Edmond Edmond		
Enid Enid		
Fairview Fairview		
Indiahoma Post Oak		
Lawton Faith Bible		
Okeene Okeene		
Tulsa Parkside		
Weatherford Pine Acres	15	2,593
General Conference Mennonite		
Canton Zion		
Carnegie Greenfield		

Clinton	First		
Clinton	Koinonia		
Cordell	Herald		
Deer Creek	Deer Creek		
Enid	Grace		
Hammon	Bethel		
Hydro	Bethel		
Inola	Eden		
Medford	Medford		
Meno	New Hopedale		
Oklahoma City	Joy		
Ringwood	West New Hopedale		
Seiling	Indian		
Stillwater	Fellowship		
Turpin	Turpin	17	1,174
Church of God in Christ, Mennonite			
Chickasha	Plainview		
Fairview	Fairview		
Goltry	Pleasant View		
Weatherford	Cedar	4	449
Mennonite Church Conference			
Adair	Oak Grove		
Hydro	Pleasant View		
Pryor	Zion	3	368
Old Order Amish District			
Chouteau	Northeast		
Chouteau	Northwest		
Chouteau	Southeast		
Clarita	Clarita		
Inola	Inola		
Inola	Southwest	6	365
Brethren in Christ			
Leedey	Red Star		
Oklahoma City	Oklahoma City		
Thomas	Bethany	3	241
Kleine Gemeinde			
Boley	Kleine Gemeinde	1	65
Beachy Amish Mennonite			
Thomas	Zion	1	46
Conservative Mennonite, Unaffiliated			
Paden	Calvary	1	15
(9)	*Oklahoma Total*	*51*	*5,316*

Oregon

		Congregations	*Members*
Dual Conference (Pacific Northwest GC/MC)			
Albany	Albany		
Albany	Bethany		
Aurora	Calvary		
Canby	Pacific Covenant		
Clackamos	Sunrise		
Corvallis	Prince of Peace		
Crooked River Ranch	Ranch Chapel		
Dallas	Grace		
Eugene	Eugene		
Hubbard	Zion		
Lebanon	Lebanon		
Logsden	Neighborhood		
McMinnville	First		
Portland	Peace		
Portland	Portland		
Salem	Salem		
Salem	Western		
Shedd	Plainview		
Sweet Home	River of Life		
Woodburn	Iglesia Pentacostas	20	2,237
Mennonite Brethren			
Dallas	Dallas		
Eugene	North Park		
Grants Pass	Grants Pass		
Hillsboro	Iglesia Cristiana		
Milwaukie	Slavic Evangelical		
Portland	Primera Ebenezer		
Portland	Slavic Christian		
Salem	Kingwood Bible		
Salem	Slavic Christian	9	1,464
Mennonite Church, Unaffiliated			
Albany	Fairview		
Corvallis	Fellowship		
Hubbard	Hopewell		
Lebanon	New Hope		
McMinnville	True Vine		
McMinnville	Iglesia Principe de Paz		
Milwaukie	Iglesia de Restauracion		
Sweet Home	Sweet Home		
Toledo	Toledo		
Winston	Winston	10	753

Mennonite Church Independent Conference

Brownsville	Brownsville		
Cove	Grande Ronde		
Escatada	Porter		
Sheridan	Sheridan		
Tangent	Tangent	5	354

Brethren in Christ

Grants Pass	Redwood Country		
Salem	Hispanic Group		
Salem	Pacific Highway	3	139

Church of God in Christ, Mennonite

Scio	Evergreen	1	108

Amish Mennonite

Harrisburg	Harrisburg	1	88
(7)	*Oregon Total*	49	5,143

Pennsylvania

		Congregations	*Members*

Mennonite Church, Lancaster Conference

Adamstown	Gehman
Akron	Pilgrims
Allentown	Iglesia Ebenezer
Alsace Manor	Alsace Manor
Berwyn	Kapatiran Christian
Bethel	Meckville
Bethlehem	Community
Bird-in-Hand	Stumptown
Blandon	Blandon
Bowmansville	Bowmansville
Bradford	Bradford
Camp Hill	Slate Hill
Canton	Canton
Carbondale	Fellowship
Chester	Way Through Christ
Christiana	Andrews Bridge
Churchtown	Churchtown
Coatesville	Coatesville
Coatesville	Newlinville
Cocolamus	Lauver
Columbia	Chestnut Hill

Columbia	Columbia
Conestoga	River Corner
Danville	Derry
Denver	Red Run
Downingtown	Cornerstone
Downingtown	Downing Hills
East Earl	Lichty
East Earl	Weaverland
East Petersburg	East Petersburg
East Salem	Delaware
Eddystone	Praise Center
Elizabethtown	Bossler
Elizabethtown	Cedar Hill
Elizabethtown	Elizabethtown
Elizabethtown	Good
Elizabethtown	Risser
Ephrata	Ephrata
Ephrata	Hinkletown
Ephrata	Indiantown
Ephrata	Metzler
Ephrata	New Life
Frazer	Frazer
Gap	Millwood
Goodville	Goodville
Halifax	Halifax
Harrisburg	Cristo la Requesta
Harrisburg	Herr Street
Harrisburg	Locust Lane
Harrisburg	Peace Chapel
Hershey	Stauffer
Honey Brook	Cambridge
Kennett Square	Kennett Square
Kinzers	Hershey
Kinzers	Kinzer
Kinzers	Meadville
Lancaster	Blossom Hill
Lancaster	Charlotte Street
Lancaster	Christ the King
Lancaster	Covenant
Lancaster	El Buen Pastor
Lancaster	East Chestnut Street
Lancaster	Ethiopian Fellowship
Lancaster	First Deaf
Lancaster	Home
Lancaster	Landis Valley
Lancaster	Laurel Street

Lancaster	Lyndon
Lancaster	Mellinger
Lancaster	Rossmere
Lancaster	South Christian Street
Lancaster	Sunnyside
Lancaster	Witmer Heights
Landisville	Landisville
Lebanon	Gingerich
Lebanon	Fellowship
Lebanon	Luz de Salvacion
Leola	Groffdale
Leola	Millport
Lewisburg	Buffalo
Lincoln University	Lincoln University
Lititz	Erb
Lititz	Hammer Creek
Lititz	Hess
Lititz	Lititz
Manchester	Christian Community
Manheim	Erisman
Manheim	Grace
Manheim	Hernley
Manheim	Kauffman
Manheim	Manheim
Marietta	Community Chapel
Marietta	Marietta
Martindale	Martindale
Middletown	Fountain of Life
Middletown	Strickler
Millersville	Millersville
Millersville	University Fellowship
Milton	Community
Monroeton	West Franklin
Morris Run	Calvary
Mount Joy	Mount Joy
Mountaintop	Cornerstone
Mountville	Habecker
Mountvillle	Mountville
Myerstown	Myerstown
Nanticoke	Nanticoke
Nazareth	Maranatha Family
New Danville	New Danville
New Holland	New Holland
New Holland	New Holland Spanish
New Holland	Village Chapel
New Holland	Welsh Mountain

New Providence	Living Stones
New Providence	New Providence
Newville	Diller
Oakland Mills	Lost Creek
Oxford	Mount Vernon
Palmyra	East Hanover
Paradise	Mount Pleasant
Paradise	Nickel Pines
Paradise	Paradise
Parkesburg	Parkesburg
Pen Argyl	Bender
Philadelphia	Abundant Life Chinese
Philadelphia	Arca de Salvacion
Philadelphia	Cambodian
Philadelphia	Christian Life
Philadelphia	Diamond Street
Philadelphia	Love Truth Chinese
Philadelphia	New Mercies
Philadelphia	Northeast Fellowship
Philadelphia	Oxford Circle
Philadelphia	Palabra de Vida
Philadelphia	South Philadelphia
Philadelphia	Vietnamese
Pine Grove	Roedersville
Port Trevorton	Susquehanna
Pottsville	Palo Alto
Quarryville	Mechanic Grove
Quarryville	Oak Shade
Rawlinsville	Rawlinsville
Reading	Buttonwood
Reading	Fairview
Reading	Hampden
Reading	Luz Verdadera
Reading	Shiloh
Reading	South Seventh Street
Rebersburg	Valley
Reeders	Springs of Living Water
Reinholds	Blainsport
Richfield	Cross Roads
Rohrerstown	Rohrerstown
Schaefferstown	Krall
Schubert	Schubert
South Avis	Praise Center
Steelton	Steelton
Stevens	Faith
Stevens	Living Water

Strasburg	Strasburg		
Talmage	Carpenter		
Trout Run	Mountain View		
Turbotville	Beaver Run		
Upland	Lighthouse		
Upland	Luz de Faro		
Upper Darby	Ethiopian		
Washington Boro	Masonville		
Watsontown	East District		
Wernersville	Green Terrace		
Wheelerville	Wheelerville		
White Horse	Old Road		
Williamsport	Agape		
Willow Street	Byerland		
Willow Street	Willow Street		
Womelsdorf	Womelsdorf		
York	Stoney Brook		
York	Tidings of Peace	177	17,424

Mennonite Church, Franconia Conference

Allentown	Allentown
Allentown	El Calvario
Allentown	Vietnamese Gospel
Ambler	Ambler
Bally	Bally
Bethlehem	Steel City
Blooming Glen	Blooming Glen
Boyertown	Boyertown
Bristol	New Beginnings
Canadensis	Spruce Lake
Doylestown	Doylestown
East Athens	New Life
East Greenville	Shalom
Easton	Easton
Fleetwood	Living Word
Forksville	Living Hope
Franconia	Franconia
Frederick	Frederick
Harleysville	Salford
Kulpsville	Towamencin
Lansdale	Covenant
Lansdale	Plains
Line Lexington	Line Lexington
Morris	Bible Felowship
Newtown	Church of the Servant
Norristown	Methacton
Norristown	New Life

Pennsburg	Finland		
Perkasie	Deep Run East		
Perkasie	Perkasie		
Perkiomenville	Perkiomenville		
Pottstown	Estrella de la Manana		
Quakertown	Rocky Ridge		
Quakertown	Swamp		
Royersford	Word of Joy		
Schwenksville	Hersteins		
Shelly	Salem		
Skippack	Upper Skippack		
Souderton	Souderton		
Spring City	Vincent		
Spring Mount	Spring Mount		
Susquehanna	Lakeview		
Telford	Rockhill		
Tunkhannok	Tunkhannok		
Whitehall	Whitehall		
Yerkes	Providence	46	6,643

Mennonite Church, Atlantic Coast Conference

Atglen	Maple Grove
Bart	Bart
Birdsboro	Zion
Boyertown	Ark Bible
Christiana	Christiana
Coatesville	Sandy Hill
East Earl	Bethany
Fleetwood	Hope Community
Gettysburg	Bethel
Gordonville	Ridgeview
Greencastle	Cedar Grove
Honey Brook	Rockville
Leola	Forest Hills
Morgantown	Conestoga
Neffsville	Neffsville
Oley	Oley
Oxford	Media
Port Allegany	Birch Grove
Warfordsburg	Black Oak
York	Zion

Hopewell District

Adamstown	Good Shepherd
Bernville	Hopewell
Berwyn	Hopewell
Birdsboro	LOVE
Downingtown	New Life

Elverson	Hopewell		
Manheim	Immanuel		
New Holland	Petra		
Pottstown	Hopewell		
Reading	Hopewell		
Souderton	Hopewell		
Spring City	Fellowship	32	4,907

Mennonite Church, Allegheny Conference

Allensville	Allensville		
Altoona	Canan Station		
Altoona	Cornerstone		
Altoona	Mill Run		
Barrville	Barrville		
Beaver Springs	Manbeck		
Belleville	Maple Grove		
Belleville	Rockville		
Davidsville	Carpenter Park		
Holsopple	Blough		
Holsopple	Kaufman		
Holsopple	Thomas		
Johnstown	First		
Johnstown	Stahl		
Johnstown	Weaver		
Martinsburg	Martinsburg		
Masontown	Masontown		
Mattawana	Mattawana		
Middleburg	Boyer		
Mount Union	Otelia		
Pittsburgh	Pittsburgh		
Scottdale	Kingview		
Scottdale	Scottdale		
Seanor	Seanor		
Somerset	New Life		
Springs	Springs		
State College	University		
Woodbury	Cove	28	2,857

Mennonite Church, Franklin Conference

Chambersburg	Cedar Street
Chambersburg	Chambersburg
Chambersburg	Pleasant View
Chambersburg	Pond Bank
Chambersburg	Zion Covenant
Greencastle	Salem Ridge
Marion	Marion
McConnellsburg	Rock Hill
Mercersburg	Mercersburg

Shippensburg	Living Faith		
Warfordsburg	Bethel		
Waynesboro	Fairview		
Willow Hill	Shady Pine	13	1,322

Mennonite Church, Ohio Conference

Conneaut Lake	Sunnyside		
Corry	Beaverdam		
New Castle	Maple Grove		
Spartansburg	Valley View	4	333
	Total	288	32,102

Old Order Amish Districts

Allensville	Upper East
Allensville	Upper West
Allenwood	White Deer Valley
Atlantic	Crawford West
Atlantic	Northeast
Atlantic	Southeast
Bart	Bart
Belleville	Belleville
Belleville	Lower
Belleville	Lower Middle
Belleville	Upper Middle
Belleville	Whitehall
Berlin	Stoney Creek
Bird-in-Hand	Bird-in-Hand
Bird-in-Hand	East Weavertown
Bird-in-Hand	Northwest Upper Millcreek
Bird-in-Hand	Stumptown Road
Bird-in-Hand	West Millcreek
Bird-in-Hand	West Weavertown
Blain	West Perry
Centerville	Buells Corner South
Centerville	Centerville
Centerville	Centerville West
Christiana	Cooperville
Christiana	East Smyrna
Christiana	Nine Points East
Christiana	Nine Points West
Christiana	North Cream
Christiana	South Georgetown
Christiana	Southwest Nine Points
Christiana	Steelville
Christiana	West Smyrna
Clintonville	Clintonville

Clintonville	Clintonville West
Coatesville	Compass
Danville	Valley
Dayton	Dayton
Delta	York County
Delta	York West
Dornsife	Northumberland
Drumore	North
Drumore	South
Dry Run	Path Valley East
Dry Run	Path Valley Middle
Dry Run	Path Valley North
Dry Run	Path Valley South
Elizabethville	West Dauphin
Enon Valley	Enon Valley
Fredonia	Fredonia
Fredonia	North
Gap	Buena Vista
Gap	Gap
Gap	Lower Pequea Gap
Gap	Lower Pequea Millwood
Gap	North Mount Vernon
Gap	North Whitehorse
Gap	Salisbury Heights
Gap	South Spring Garden
Gap	South Whitehorse
Gordonville	Cattail
Gordonville	East Centerville
Gordonville	East Hatville
Gordonville	Newport
Gordonville	Northwest Lower Pequea
Gordonville	Southeast Groffdale
Gordonville	Southeast Lower Millcreek
Gordonville	South Middle Pequea
Gordonville	West Centerville
Gratz	Crossroad
Guys Mills	Guys Mills East
Guys Mills	Guys Mills Southwest
Guys Mills	Guys Mills West
Honey Brook	Beaver Dam
Honey Brook	North Honey Brook
Honey Brook	South Honey Brook
Honey Brook	West Honey Brook
Howard	Little Nittany
Howard	West Nittany
Intercourse	East Intercourse

Intercourse	North Intercourse
Intercourse	South Intercourse
Kinzers	North Kinzers
Kinzers	North Spring Garden
Kinzers	South Kinzers
Kinzers	Springville
Kirkwood	Middle Kirkwood
Kirkwood	North Kirkwood
Kirkwood	North Union
Kirkwood	South Kirkwood
Kirkwood	South Union
Kirkwood	West Kirkwood
Lancaster	Greenland
Lancaster	Rocky Springs
Lancaster	West Upper Millcreek
Landisburg	East Perry
Leola	Leola
Leola	Mechanicsburg
Leola	Northeast Millcreek
Leola	Southwest Groffdale
Leola	Upper Millcreek
Lewisburg	Buffalo Valley
Linesville	Linesville
Lititz	Hammer Creek
Lititz	Lititz
Lititz	West Lititz
Loganton	Sugar Valley East
Loganton	Sugar Valley Middle
Loganton	Sugar Valley West
Marion Center	Ambrose North
Marion Center	Ambrose South
Mercer	Middle
Mercer	South
Meyersdale	Pocohantas
Meyersdale	Summit Mills
Mifflintown	East Salem
Mifflintown	North
Mifflintown	South
Mifflintown	Van Wert
Millersburg	Lykens Valley
Mill Hall	Mackeyville
Mill Hall	East Nittany
Montgomery	East White Deer Valley
Mount Joy	Mount Joy
Myerstown	East
Myerstown	North

Myerstown	West
Narvon	Cains
Narvon	Conestoga
Narvon	North Lower Pequea
Narvon	Northeast Pequea
Narvon	West Conestoga
Newburg	Cumberland Valley
Newburg	East Cumberland Valley
Newburg	North Cumberland Valley
New Holland	Lower Millcreek
New Holland	Meadville
New Holland	Northeast Groffdale
New Holland	Northeast Lower Millcreek
New Holland	Northwest Groffdale
New Providence	New Providence
New Providence	South New Providence
New Wilmington	East
New Wilmington	Middle North
New Wilmington	Middle South
New Wilmington	North
New Wilmington	Northeast
New Wilmington	Northeast II
New Wilmington	Northwest
New Wilmington	Northwest II
New Wilmington	South
New Wilmington	Southwest
New Wilmington	West
Nottingham	Nottingham
Oxford	South Cream
Oxford	Oxford
Paradise	Belmont
Paradise	Iva
Paradise	Nickel Mines
Paradise	Northeast Georgetown
Paradise	Paradise
Paradise	South Georgetown
Paradise	West Georgetown
Parkesburg	South Mount Vernon
Punxsutawney	Middle
Punxsutawney	North
Punxsutawney	Southwest
Quarryville	Ashville
Quarryville	Fairmont
Quarryville	Greentree
Quarryville	Mechanics Grove
Quarryville	Mount Pleasant

Quarryville	Quarryville
Quarryville	South Beaver Creek
Quarryville	South Greentree
Rebersburg	Brush Valley East
Rebersburg	Brush Valley West
Rebersburg	Rebersburg
Rome	Bradford
Ronks	East Weavertown
Ronks	Fairview
Ronks	Ronks
Ronks	Southeast Millcreek
Ronks	Upper Middle Pequea
Ronks	Upper Pequea
Ronks	West Lower Millcreek
Saegertown	Hostetler
Salisbury	Middle
Salisbury	Niverton
Smicksburg	Mahoning
Smicksburg	Middle
Smicksburg	Middle North
Smicksburg	Middle South
Smicksburg	Middle Southeast
Smicksburg	Smicksburg South
Smoketown	Smoketown
Soudersburg	Soudersburg
Spartansburg	Britton Run East
Spartansburg	Britton Run West
Spartansburg	Buells Corner North
Spartansburg	Spartansburg East
Spartansburg	Spartansburg East II
Spartansburg	Spartansburg West
Spring Glen	East Dauphin
Springs	Springs
Strasburg	Beaver Creek
Strasburg	Edisonville
Strasburg	Northeast Beaver Creek
Strasburg	Northwest
Strasburg	West Beaver Creek
Sugar Grove	Sugar Grove East
Sugar Grove	Sugar Grove Middle East
Sugar Grove	Sugar Grove West
Talmage	Talmage
Townville	Townville
Trade City	East
Trade City	North
Trade City	West

Tyrone	Sinking Valley		
Ulysses	Ulysses		
Union City	Union City		
Vintage	Vintage		
Volant	Southeast		
Volant	Volant		
Wakefield	East Wakefield		
Wakefield	Wakefield		
Washingtonville	Washingtonville		
Williamsport	Nipponese		
Witmer	East Witmer		
Witmer	West Witmer	230	14,835

Brethren in Christ

Akron	New Joy
Belleville	Big Valley
Berwick	Hunlock Creek
Blairs Mills	Blairs Mills
Blandburg	Blandburg
Breezewood	Mountain Chapel
Carlisle	Carlisle
Centre Hall	Colyer
Chambersburg	Air Hill
Chambersburg	Antrim
Chambersburg	Chambersburg
Chambersburg	New Guilford
Chambersburg	West Side
Cleona	Fairland
Collegeville	Perkiomen Valley
Dillsburg	Cumberland Valley
Dillsburg	Dillsburg
Downingtown	Marsh Creek
Duncannon	Roseglen
East Berlin	Morning Hour
Elizabethtown	Bright Hope
Elizabethtown	Conoy
Elizabethtown	Elizabethtown
Elliottsburg	Pleasant Valley
Enola	West Shore
Everett	Clear Creek
Everett	Eight Square Chapel
Everett	Springhope
Fairfield	Iron Springs
Gettysburg	Peace Light
Grantham	Grantham
Hanover	Hanover
Harrisburg	Harrisburg

Harrisburg	Skyline View
Hershey	Hershey
Hollidaysburg	Canoe Creek
Hopewell	Shermans Valley
Howard	Marsh Creek
Hummelstown	Hummelstown
Ickesburg	Saville
Lancaster	Hempfield
Lancaster	Lancaster
Lancaster	Pequea
Lewistown	Granville
Linglestown	New Hope
Lititz	Speedwell Heights
Llewellyn	Llewellyn
Manheim	Manheim
Martinsburg	Martinsburg
Mastersonville	Mastersonville
Maytown	Maytown
McVeytown	Ferguson Valley
McVeytown	Newton Hamilton
Mechanicsburg	Mechanicsburg
Mechanicsburg	Messiah Village
Mechanicsburg	New Song
Mercersburg	Montgomery
Mercersburg	Mount Tabor
Mifflintown	Cedar Grove
Mill Hall	Cedar Heights
Millersburg	Free Grace
Millersville	Millersville
Montoursville	Montoursville
Mount Holly Springs	Wesley
Mount Joy	Cross Roads
Mount Joy	Mount Pleasant
Mountville	Manor
Newburg	Mowersville
New Cumberland	Fairview
New Holland	Summit View
Newville	Green Spring
Palmyra	Palmyra
Philadelphia	Circle of Hope
Red Lion	Pleasant View
Refton	Refton
Reinholds	Bethel Springs
Roxbury	Blue Mountain
Saxton	Saxton
Selinsgrove	Susquehana Valley

Sellersville	New Covenant		
Shippensburg	Mount Rock		
Shippensburg	South Mountain Chapel		
Silverdale	Silverdale		
Souderton	Souderton		
Spring Mills	Green Grove		
Stowe	Stowe		
Three Springs	Center Grove		
Tremont	Tremont		
Waynesboro	Fairview Avenue		
Waynesboro	Five Forks		
Waynesboro	Hollowell		
Westfield	Jemison Valley		
York	Locust Grove		
York Haven	Redland Valley	94	12,497

Mennonite Church Independent Conferences

Adamstown	Open Door
Allen	Churchtown
Bernville	Bernville
Blue Ball	Blue Ball
Cambridge Springs	French Creek
Chambersburg	Calvary
Chambersburg	Culbertson
Chambersburg	Upper Strasburg
Cochranton	Pleasant View
Cornwall	Miners Village
Danville	Danville
Denver	Denver
Denver	Muddy Creek
Doylesburg	Burns Valley
East Berlin	Kralltown
Ephrata	Pleasant Valley
Fredericksburg	Little Mountain
Gap	Simmontown
Gettysburg	Mummasburg
Grantville	Providence
Greencastle	Antrim
Hanover	Bairs Hostetters
Hanover	Hanover
Hartleton	Hartleton
Hereford	Chapel
Honey Brook	Honey Brook
Jonestown	Shirksville
Lancaster	Conestoga Drive
Lebanon	Dohner
Lebanon	Elm Street

Lebanon	Sharon		
Leola	Leola		
Lititz	New Haven		
Manheim	White Oak		
Martindale	Centerville		
McConnellsburg	Mountain View		
Menges Mill	Garber		
Millerstown	Millerstown		
Millersville	Blue Rock		
Millmont	Millmont		
Mount Holly Springs	Mountain View		
Mount Pleasant Mills	Shade Mountain		
Myerstown	Fair Haven		
Myerstown	Lebanon Valley		
Myerstown	Swatara		
Newville	Blue Ridge		
North East	Lakeview		
Orwin	Orwin		
Philadelphia	Sixth Street		
Port Royal	Port Royal		
Quarryville	Bethel		
Refton	Refton		
Rheems	Rheems		
Richland	Richland		
Robesonia	Texter Mountain		
Schaefferstown	Schaefferstown		
Schoeneck	Valley View		
Shippensburg	Rowe		
Strodes Mills	Strodes Mills		
Tamaqua	New England Valley		
Telford	Indian Creek		
Thomasville	Hershey		
Thompsontown	Goodwill		
Ulster	Union Valley		
Waynesboro	Waynecastle		
Woodbury	Woodbury		
York	North Hartman Street		
York Springs	Latimore	68	5,225

General Conference Mennonite

Allentown	First
Bally	Hereford
Bedminster	Deep Run West
Bowmansville	Pine Grove
Coopersburg	Saucon
Fairfield	Fairfield
Harleysville	Indian Valley

Holland	Good Samaritan		
Huntington Valley	First		
Lancaster	Bethel		
Lansdale	Grace		
Mifflintown	Cornerstone		
Philadelphia	Comunidad de Amor		
Philadelphia	Second		
Quakertown	East Swamp		
Quakertown	Springfield		
Quakertown	United		
Quakertown	West Swamp		
Reinholds	Emmanuel		
Richfield	Richfield		
Roaring Spring	Roaring Spring		
Schwenksville	Eden		
Skippack	Lower Skippack		
Souderton	Zion		
Zionsville	Upper Milford	25	4,580

Old Order Mennonite, Weaverland Conference

Alinda	Milltown		
Bethel	Bethel		
Bowmansville	Bowmansville		
Churchtown	Churchtown		
East Earl	Weaverland		
Ephrata	Fairmount Home		
Ephrata	Meadow Valley		
Ephrata	South Hinkletown		
Ephrata	Springville		
Gordonville	Pequea		
Lebanon	Mountain View		
Leola	Groffdale		
Lititz	Lime Rock		
Manheim	Clearview		
Martindale	Martindale		
Meiserville	County Line		
Myerstown	Fairview		
Myerstown	Martin's		
Myerstown	Mount Zion		
Newville	Oakville		
Quarryville	Fairmount		
Walnuttown	Walnuttown	22	3,868

Old Order Mennonite, Groffdale Conference

Bowmansville	Bowmansville		
Churchtown	Churchtown		
Denver	Muddy Creek		
East Earl	Weaverland		

Ephrata	Conestoga		
Fleetwood	Fleetwood		
Kutztown	Center		
Leola	Groffdale		
Lititz	Millway		
Martindale	Martindale		
Martinsburg	Martinsburg		
Martinsburg	Piney Creek		
Mifflinburg	Mountain View		
New Enterprise	New Enterprise		
New Holland	New Holland		
Shippensburg	Clearfield		
Shippensburg	Meadow View		
Shippensburg	Shippensburg		
Terre Hill	Spring Grove		
Vicksburg	Vicksburg	20	3,270

Beachy Amish Mennonite

Belleville	Pleasant View		
Belleville	Valley View		
Bird in Hand	Weavertown		
Gap	Gapview		
Gap	Mine Road		
Guys Mills	Plainview		
Hadley	Maple Grove		
McAlvey's Fort	Shavers Creek		
Middleburg	Shekeinah		
Mifflin	Shade Mountain		
Mifflinburg	Shady Grove		
New Holland	Summitview		
New Holland	Westhaven		
Salisbury	Mountain View		
Somerset	Somerset		
Vicksburg	Vicksburg		
White Horse	Pequea	17	1,778

Mennonite Church, Unaffiliated

Belleville	Beth-El
Coatesville	New Hope
Ephrata	New Covenant
Harleysville	Living Faith
Lancaster	Bridgeport
Lancaster	Followers of Jesus
Lancaster	House of the Lord
Lansdale	Lansdale
Lebanon	North Lebanon
Lititz	Shiloh
Manheim	Mount Hope

Masontown	Evangelical		
McClure	Beaver Springs		
Morgantown	Community		
Philadelphia	Bethany House		
Philadelphia	Holiness		
Quakertown	Haycock		
Sandy Lake	Berea		
Schellsburg	Pleasant View		
Shippensburg	Shippensburg		
Stevens	Vineyard	21	1,229

United Zion Churches

Akron	Akron		
Annville	Annville		
Elizabethtown	Elizabethtown		
Ephrata	Ephrata		
Ephrata	Hahnstown		
Lebanon	Mission		
Lebanon	Moonshine Township		
Lititz	Home		
Manheim	Pleasant View		
Newmanstown	Haaks		
Palmyra	Palmyra		
Reinholds	Reinholds		
Stevens	Stevens	13	856

Dual Conference (GC/MC)

Akron	Akron		
Lancaster	Community		
Philadelphia	Germantown		
Philadelphia	West Philadelphia	4	716

Old Order Amish, Nebraska Group

Aaronsburg	Penns Valley 2		
Barrville	Barrville		
Belleville	Long Lane		
Belleville	Woodland Middle		
McClure	McClure		
McClure	McClure No. 2		
Milroy	Church Lane		
Milroy	East Milroy		
Milroy	South Milroy		
Reedsville	Reedsville		
Reedsville	Woodland West		
Three Springs	Penns Valley 1		
Winfield	Winfield	13	715

Conservative Mennonite Conference

Belleville	Locust Grove		
Cochranton	Bethel		

Crenshaw	Crenshaw		
Reedsville	Mountain View		
Salisbury	Oak Dale	5	530

Mennonite Fellowship Churches

Blooming Valley	Blooming Valley		
Ephrata	Grace		
Fayetteville	Spring Valley		
Lebanon	Royers		
Lynnville	Blue Mountain		
Mount Pleasant Mills	Bethel		
New Bethlehem	New Bethlehem		
Newville	Stoughstown		
Stoney Fork	Stoney Fork		
Three Springs	Meadow Green	10	509

Old Order Mennonite, Stauffer Group

Ephrata	Pike		
Port Trevorton	Lower District		
Port Trevorton	Upper District	3	471

Anabaptist Christian Fellowship

Lebanon	Hope		
Leola	Charity		
Shippensburg	Shippensburg	3	365

Church of God in Christ, Mennonite

Belleville	Rock Haven		
Fleetwood	Fleetwood		
Mifflinburg	Morning Star		
Shippensburg	Living Faith	4	355

Mennonite Christian Fellowship

Bedford	Christian Light		
Cochranton	Pilgrim		
Hillsdale	Hillsdale		
McVeytown	Gospel Light		
Pine Grove	Pine Grove		
Saint Thomas	Emmanuel	6	299

New Order Amish

Conneautville	Conneaut East		
Conneautville	Conneaut West		
Gap	Limeville		
Honey Brook	Honey Brook		
Jamestown	Jamestown	5	281

Reidenbach Old Order Mennonite

Bowmansville	House Church		
Danville	Montour County		
Ephrata	House Church I		
Ephrata	House Church II		
Ephrata	House Church III		

Ephrata	Reidenbach		
Ephrata	Reidenbach West		
New Holland	House Church	8	280
Old Order Mennonite, Unaffiliated			
Ephrata	Jonas Weaver Church		
Ephrata	Martin Weaver Church		
Port Trevorton	Aaron Martin Church		
Port Trevorton	Allen Martin Church		
Port Trevorton	Brubaker	5	257
Old Order Amish, Byler Group			
Belleville	East Byler		
Belleville	West Byler I		
Belleville	West Byler II	3	165
Old Order River Brethren			
Chambersburg	Franklin District		
Mount Joy	Lancaster District	2	156
Mennonite/Church of the Brethren			
Lancaster	ACTS Covenant	1	129
Reformed Mennonite			
Carlisle	Middlesex		
Strasburg	Longeneckers		
Waynesboro	Waynesboro	3	123
Old Order River Brethren, Horst Group			
Chambersburg	Horst	1	105
Old Order Mennonite, John Martin Group			
New Holland	Martin	1	36
Old Order Mennonite, Hoover Group			
Port Trevorton	Noah Hoover	1	27
Old Order River Brethren, Unaffiliated			
Saint Thomas	Old Church	1	22
United Mennonite			
Lancaster	House Meetings	1	12
(31)	*Pennsylvania Grand Total*	887	87,177

Puerto Rico

		Congregations	Members
Mennonite Church Conference (Convention)			
Aibonito	Aibonito		
Aibonito	Betania		
Barranquitos	Palo Hincado		
Bayamon	Bayamon		
Caguas	Guavate		

Cayey	Cayey		
Coamo	Coamo		
La Plata	La Plata		
Orocovis	Botijas		
Ponce	Ponce		
San Juan	Summit Hills	11	530

Mennonite Church, Independent Conferences

Caribbean			
Arecibo	Asamonte		
Coamo	Evangelica		
Hatillo	Iglesia Cristiana		
Lares	Iglesia Evangelica		
Sabana Hoyes	Mantial de Vida	5	147
Southeastern			
Anasco	Followers of Christ		
Barceloneta	Fountain of Life	2	7
(3)	*Puerto Rico Total*	*18*	*684*

South Carolina

		Congregations	Members
Beachy Amish Mennonite			
Abbeville	Cold Springs		
Blackville	Calvary		
Cross Hill	Cross Hill	3	210
Mennonite Church, Unaffiliated			
Fair Play	Fair Play		
Honea Path	Whispering Pines		
Pickens	Pickens	3	188
Mennonite Church Independent Conference			
Barnwell	Barnwell	1	89
Mennonite Church Conference			
Anderson	Anderson		
Charleston	Cornerstone	2	58
Amish Mennonite, Unaffiliated			
New Holland	New Holland	1	45
(5)	*South Carolina Total*	*10*	*590*

South Dakota

		Congregations	Members
General Conference Mennonite			
Avon	Friedensberg		
Bridgewater	New Hutterthal		
Bridgewater	Zion		
Brookings	Fellowship		
Doland	Emmanuel		
Freeman	Bethany		
Freeman	Hutterthal		
Freeman	Salem		
Freeman	Salem-Zion		
Souix Falls	Good Shepherd	10	1,798
Mennonite Brethren			
Bridgewater	Salem		
Freeman	Silver Lake		
Gettysburg	Grace Bible		
Huron	Bethesda		
Onida	Emmanuel		
Pine Ridge	Gospel		
Porcupine	Lakota		
Rapid City	Bible Fellowship		
Souix Falls	Lincoln Hills		
Yale	Bethel	10	1,108
Independent Mennonite			
Carpenter	Hutterthal		
Huron	Mount Olivet		
Marion	Bethesda	3	552
Church of God in Christ, Mennonite			
Iroquois	Faith	1	122
Evangelical Mennonite Brethren			
Marion	Marion	1	90
Dual Conference (GC/MC)			
Sioux Falls	Sermon on the Mount	1	24
(6)	*South Dakota Total*	26	3,694

Tennessee

		Congregations	Members
Old Order Amish Districts			
Ethridge	East		
Ethridge	Middle		

Ethridge	Middle East		
Ethridge	North		
Ethridge	Northwest		
Ethridge	South		
Ethridge	West		
Huntington	Carroll		
Nunnelly	Hickman	9	495
Beachy Amish Mennonite			
Belvidere	Belvidere		
Cottage Grove	Bethel		
Cottage Grove	New Boston		
Whiteville	Whiteville	4	223
Brethren in Christ			
De Rossett	De Rossett		
McMinnville	Rolling Acres		
Smithville	Pomeroy Chapel	3	197
Mennonite Christian Fellowship			
Crossville	Mount Moriah		
Deer Lodge	Mount Zion		
Greeneville	Greene County		
Sparta	White County	4	189
Amish Mennonite, Unaffiliated			
Altamont	Cumberland		
Lewisburg	Marshall County		
Lynchburg	Moore County		
Olive Hill	Hardin County		
Wildersville	Rock Springs	5	161
Mennonite Church Conference			
Knoxville	Concord		
Knoxville	Knoxville		
Mountain City	Rainbow		
Nashville	Harmony	4	133
Old Order Mennonite, Unaffiliated			
Cookeville	Christian Community		
Decatur	Christian Community		
Lobelville	Crane Creek		
Lobelville	Russell Creek	4	124
Anabaptist Christian Fellowship			
Finger	Finger		
Woodbury	Grace	2	110
Church of God in Christ, Mennonite			
Lobelville	Pleasant View		
Monterey	Cumberland Mountain	2	82
Reformed Mennonite			
Oakland	House Church	1	9
(10)	*Tennessee Total*	*38*	*1,723*

Texas

		Congregations	Members
Church of God in Christ, Mennonite			
Brookston	West Haven		
Dalhart	Country Side		
Detroit	Red River Valley		
El Campo	El Campo		
Farwell	Farwell		
Texhoma	Texhoma		
Texline	Texline		
Victoria	Southern Hope	8	556
Mennonite Church Conference			
Alamo	Casa de Oracion		
Brownsville	Iglesia del Cordero		
Corpus Christi	Prince of Peace		
Edinburg	New Jerusalem		
Harlingen	Primera		
Mathis	Calvary		
Mathis	Tabernacle de Fe		
Mc Allen	Good News		
Perryton	Perryton	9	482
Old Colony Mennonite			
Seminole	Old Colony	1	339
Mennonite Brethren			
Donna	Donna		
Garciasville	Iglesia de Gracia		
Grulla	Grulla		
La Joya	La Joya		
Laredo	Iglesia Evangelica		
Mc Allen	Iglesia de Gracia		
Mission	Mission		
Palmview	Neuva Vida		
Pharr	Pharr	9	337
Dual Conference (GC/MC)			
Austin	Austin		
Dallas	Comunidad de Esperanza		
Dallas	Iglesia Cristiana		
Dallas	Peace		
Forth Worth	Hope		
Houston	Houston		
San Antonio	San Antonio	7	269
Mennonite Evangelical Churches			
Paris	Evangelical		
Seminole	Seminole	2	192

Reinlaender Mennonite Church
Seminole	Reinlaender	1	170

Evangelical Mennonite Mission Conference
Seminole	Gospel	1	154

Beachy Amish Mennonite
Grandview	Grandview		
Lott	Faith	2	87

Conservative Mennonite Conference
San Antonio	Abundant Life		
San Antonio	Fountain of Life	2	68

Mennonite Church Independent Conference
Scurry	Grays Prairie	1	39

Mennonite Brethren/Mennonite Church
Premont	United	1	35

Anabaptist Christian Fellowship
Garland	Maranatha	1	22

Mennonite Church, Unaffiliated
Canton	Church at Canton	1	16

Old Order Amish
Gonzales	Gonzales	1	13
(15)	*Texas Total*	47	2,779

Vermont

		Congregations	Members
Mennonite Church, Franconia Conference			
Bridgewater Corners	Bethany		
Essex Junction	Peace Fellowship		
Taftsville	Taftsville	3	91
Mennonite Church, Unaffiliated			
Chester	Andover	1	87
Mennonite Church, Independent Conference			
Wolcott	Wolcott	1	22
(3)	*Vermont Total*	5	200

Virginia

		Congregations	Members
Mennonite Church Conference			
Arlington	Buenas Nuevas		
Bayse	Woodland		

Broadway	Bethel
Broadway	Trissels
Broadway	Zion
Charlottesville	Charlottesville
Chesapeake	Deep Creek
Chesapeake	Mount Pleasant
Christiansburg	Christiansburg
Criders	Valley View
Dayton	Dayton
Elkton	Beldor
Falls Church	Vietnamese
Fredericksburg	Fredericksburg
Fulks Run	Gospel Hill
Fulks Run	Hebron
Grottoes	Mount Vernon
Hampton	Calvary
Harrisonburg	Agape Bilingual
Harrisonburg	Broad Street
Harrisonburg	Community
Harrisonburg	Family of Hope
Harrisonburg	Harrisonburg
Harrisonburg	Immanuel
Harrisonburg	Lindale
Harrisonburg	New Covenant
Harrisonburg	Park View
Harrisonburg	Ridgeway
Harrisonburg	Shalom
Harrisonburg	Weavers
Lyndhurst	Lynside
Mount Clinton	Mount Clinton
Mount Jackson	Mount Jackson
Newport News	Huntington
Newport News	Providence
Newport News	Warwick River
Norfolk	Word of Life
Powhatan	Powhatan
Richmond	First
Rileyville	Big Spring
Schuyler	Rehoboth
Singers Glen	Morning View
Singers Glen	Zion Hill
South Boston	Faith
Staunton	Staunton
Stephens City	Stephens City
Stuarts Draft	Greenmonte
Stuarts Draft	Stuarts Draft

Timberville	Cross Roads		
Vienna	Northern Virginia		
Virginia Beach	Landstown		
Waynesboro	Hildebrand		
Waynesboro	Mountain View		
Waynesboro	Springdale		
Waynesboro	Waynesboro		
Williamsburg	Williamsburg	56	6,317

Cornerstone Mennonite Churches

Broadway	Cornerstone		
Elkton	Cornerstone		
Mount Crawford	Cornerstone		
Port Republic	Cornerstone		
Richmond	Cornerstone		
Waynesboro	Cornerstone	6	1,012

Mennonite Church, Independent Southeastern Conference

Broadway	Bethesda		
Dayton	Bank		
Dayton	Bethany		
Harrisonburg	Pike		
Hinton	Peake		
McGaheysville	McGaheysville		
Rawley Springs	Rawley Springs		
South Boston	Ebenezer		
Stanardsville	Mount Herman	9	648

Beachy Amish Mennonite

Aroda	Oak Grove		
Catlett	Faith		
Charlottesville	Gospel Light		
Farmville	Farmville		
Free Union	Faith Mission		
Stuarts Draft	Mount Zion		
Stuarts Draft	Pilgrim		
Virginia Beach	Kempsville	8	532

Old Order Mennonite, Virginia Groffdale Conference

Dayton	Oak Grove		
Dayton	Pleasant View		
Dayton	Riverdale	3	426

Brethren in Christ

Accomac	Calvary		
Callaway	Adney Gap		
Dublin	Highland Park		
Harrisonburg	Dayspring		
Hillsville	Bethel		
Lynchburg	Lynchburg		
Roanoke	Ridge View		

Winchester	Winchester	8	320

Old Order Mennonite, Wenger Group

Dayton	Oak Grove		
Dayton	Pleasant View	2	273

Mennonite Church, Unaffiliated

Floyd	Floyd County		
Cumberland	Cumberland		
Gladys	Bethel		
Harrisonburg	Calvary		
Stanley	Lucas Hollow		
Timberville	Timberville	6	252

Mennonite Fellowship Churches

Amelia	Pilgrim		
Dayton	Pleasant Valley	2	160

Old Order Mennonite, Weaverland Conference

Dayton	Mount Pleasant	1	95

Old Order Amish Districts

Abingdon	Abingdon		
Pearisburg	Walker Mountain		
Pearisburg	White Gate		
Tazewell	Burkes Garden	4	92

Conservative Mennonite Conference

Catlett	Dayspring		
Virginia Beach	Providence	2	75

Dual Conference (GC/MC)

Richmond	Richmond	1	26
(13)	*Virginia Total*	*108*	*10,228*

Washington

		Congregations	Members

Mennonite Brethren

Bellingham	Community		
Bellingham	Slavic		
Blaine	Birch Bay		
Ferndale	Good News		
Seattle	First Ukranian		
Seattle	Slavic Missionary		
Spokane	Slavic Christian		
Vancouver	Slavic Evangelical	8	2,481

Dual Conference (Pacific Northwest GC/MC)

Bellevue	Evergreen		
Ephrata	Columbia Basin		

Federal Way	Tiawanese Trinity		
Newport	Spring Valley		
Ritzville	Menno		
Seattle	Seattle		
Spokane	Shalom		
Warden	Warden	8	496
Church of God in Christ, Mennonite			
Othelllo	Columbia River		
Tonasket	Tonasket	2	79
Mennonite Church, Independent Conference			
Chewelah	Colville Valley	1	11
(4)	*Washington Total*	*19*	*3,067*

West Virginia

		Congregations	Members
Mennonite Church Conference			
Baker	Salem		
Belington	Lambert		
Dryfork	Laneville		
Fort Seybert	Pleasant Grove		
Harman	Riverside		
Hillsboro	Church of the Mountains		
Mathias	Cove		
Mathias	Mathias		
Philippi	Philippi		
Wardensville	Crest Hill	10	219
Church of the Brethren/Mennonite			
Morgantown	Morgantown	1	110
Mennonite Church, Independent Southeastern Conference			
Bartow	Boyer Hill		
Onego	Brushy Run		
Seneca Rocks	North Fork	3	109
Brethren in Christ			
Bunker Hill	Bunker Hill	1	61
Mennonite Christian Fellowship			
Gap Mills	Gap Mills	1	53
(5)	*West Virginia Total*	*16*	*552*

Wisconsin

Congregations   Members

Old Order Amish Districts

Amherst	Portage North
Amherst	Portage South
Athens	Athens
Augusta	Augusta Northeast
Augusta	Augusta Southeast
Augusta	Augusta South Middle
Augusta	Augusta Southwest
Augusta	Augusta West
Blair	Northside
Blair	Southside
Bloomington	Bloomington
Bonduel	Bonduel
Brodhead	Brodhead
Cambria	Kingston Southeast
Cashton	East
Cashton	Middle
Cashton	Middle South
Cashton	Northwest
Cashton	West
Cazenovia	Ironton
Chaseburg	Chaseburg
Chetek	Chetek
Clear Lake	Clear Lake
Curtiss	South
Dalton	Kingston East
Durand	Clear Creek
Durand	East
Granton	Granton Northeast
Granton	Granton West
Greenwood	Greenwood
Hillsboro	Hillsboro Middle
Hillsboro	Hillsboro Northeast
Hillsboro	Hillsboro Southeast
Hillsboro	Hillsboro West
Kingston	Kingston Northwest
LaValle	LaValle
Loganville	Loganville
Loyal	Loyal East
Loyal	Loyal West
Marion	Marion
Medford	Northeast
Medford	Northwest

Mondovi	Mondovi West		
Monroe	Monroe		
New Glarus	New Glarus		
New Holstein	New Holstein		
Norwalk	Northeast		
Ontario	Valley East		
Owen	Owen-Unity		
Pardeeville	Kingston Southwest		
Readstown	Readstown I		
Readstown	Readstown II		
Rising Sun	Rising Sun		
Viroqua	Viroqua		
Wautoma	Wautoma East		
Wautoma	Wautoma West		
Westby	Middle West		
Westby	South		
Wilton	North		
Wilton	North Center		
Wilton	South		
Wilton	Valley		
Wilton	West	63	3,535
Church of God in Christ, Mennonite			
Almena	Gospel		
Barron	Barron		
Barron	Hillcrest	3	388
Mennonite Fellowship Churches			
Athens	Athens		
Augusta	Augusta		
Thorp	Thorp		
Tony	Shiloh		
Unity	Unity		
Wautoma	Oak Ridge	6	301
Old Order Mennonite, Groffdale Conference			
Curtiss	Sunny Ridge		
Longwood	Longwood		
Withee	Meadow Brook	3	190
Mennonite Church, Independent Conference			
Hayward	Northwoods		
Richland Center	Buck Creek		
Stratford	Bethany	3	129
Mennonite Church Conference			
Exeland	Exeland		
Glen Flora	South Lawrence		
Stone Lake	Sand Lake	3	107
Amish Mennonite			
Muscoda	Pleasant Valley	1	83

New Order Amish

Spencer	Spencer	1	81

Dual Conference (GC/MC)

Madison	Madison		
Waukesha	Maple Avenue	2	79

Mennonite Church, Unaffiliated

Conrath	Wayside		
Sparta	Sparta		
Stone Lake	Grace		
Wausau	The Sheepfold	4	78

Old Order Mennonite, Weaverland Conference

Granton	Pine Grove	1	71

Anabaptist Christian Fellowship

Richland Center	Gospel Light	1	70

Brethren in Christ

Sheboygan	Sheboygan		
Waukesha	New Vision	2	53

Conservative Mennonite, Unaffiliated

Sheldon	Sheldon Conservative	1	41

(14)	*Wisconsin Total*	*94*	*5,206*

Wyoming

		Congregation	Members
Mennonite Fellowship Church			
Carpenter	High Prairie	1	17

Author's Personal Summary

You and I, reader and writer, have shared an adventure together in previous pages. We have looked at the European beginnings of the Anabaptist-Mennonites, and the early establishment and current status of our clustered and scattered communities and settlements over the national scene.

We have found the contemporary Anabaptist-Mennonites spread across a broad spectrum of doctrine, practices, religious conviction, and theological thought. I had written earlier that Menno Simons is best known for his writings. Allow me to remind all of us that his favorite and most often quoted portion of scripture was from I Corinthians 3: 10 and 11: "According to the grace of God which is given unto me, as a wise masterbuilder, I have laid the foundation, and another buildeth thereon. But let every man take heed how he buildeth thereupon. For other foundation can no man lay than that is laid, which is Jesus Christ" (from the King James Version).

In our Anabaptist-Mennonite belief system today, we find many interpretations, even more than the forty-five-plus detailed in earlier sections. We can find evangelical, fundamentalist, and main-line; we find charismatics and pentecostals; we can find conformity and nonconformity, diversity and uniformity; we find activism, conservatism, liberalism, and progressivism, formal and free-style worship; and we can find negative and positive attitudes among both our leadership and membership. But regardless of the variation of our views, we should maintain a heavy balance of Christian Anabaptist concern in our congregational, family, and individual life. We are a small part of Christendom, and we must continue to strive for quality, dedication, and sacrifice, not quantity or numbers.

In our sojourn we have now brought together many ethnic groups. We have mixed our European roots and our Anglo/Dutch/ Swiss/Russian branches. We have invited Native Americans to be a part of us. We maintain a close binational relationship with our Canadian kin in the faith. We have opened our doors to Hispanics and Latinos from the Caribbean, Central America, and Mexico. We feel warm in spirit with converts and congregations of the African and Asian cultures. We are pilgrims and strangers here, passing through together. On occasion my colleagues in other denominations complimented us as a small group having a relatively high percentage of multi-cultural congregations and members.

Following are several quotes from the mid-life writings of Menno Simons. "Cease from sin; show repentance for your past lives, submit obediently to the word and will of the Lord. Believe in the Gospel, that is, believe the joyful news of divine grace through Jesus Christ. If you walk according to the spirit, and not according to the flesh, then you will become companions, citizens, children, and heirs for the new and heavenly Jerusalem." A challenge and promise to all of us to give ultimate credit to Christ.

When we count the numerous groups who claim to be Anabaptist-Mennonite, we might wonder about our variety. But our basic belief of peace and unique understanding of New Testament life from the time that Christ walked on earth until now binds us and strengthens our respect for one another. The deep convictions and new insights of certain leadership persons have caused and will create some variant congregations. But several of our larger groups are working together in joint ministries and toward merger. And as a minority-religion we are developing along with our peace witness a ministry for justice at all levels of society.

As a final summary to this report, past and present, I wish to quote again Menno Simons from one of his later-life writings, "The Prince of Peace is Jesus Christ. We who were formerly no people at all, and who knew of no peace, are now called to be...a church... of peace. Their hearts overflow with peace. Their mouths speak peace, and they walk in the way of peace."

Every Sunday the information in this book can change. New conversions and baptisms, church charters, congregational and denominational transfers, church closings, and deaths of members the previous week can influence the totals.

If you are aware of additions or deletions, changes or corrections, please advise.

Thank you!

C. Nelson Hostetter   or
31 Fulton St.   3901 Bahia Vista #412
Akron, PA 17501   Sarasota, FL 34232
(717) 859-2392   (941) 378-1473
April to October   November to March

Resources

Bender, Harold S. *These Are My People*. Herald Press.

Brechbill, Laban T. *History of the Old Order River Brethren*. Brechbill and Strickler.

Climenhaga, A.W. *History of the Brethren in Christ*. E. V. Publishing House.

Dyck, Cornelius J. *An Introduction to Mennonite History*. Herald Press.

Horst, Irvin B., ed. *Menno Simons: "Confession" and the New Birth*. Lancaster Mennonite Historical Society.

Klaasen, Walter. *Anabaptism: Neither Catholic Nor Protestant*. Conrad Press.

Lederach, Paul M. *A Third Way*. Herald Press.

Loewen, Harry and Steven Nolt. *Through Fire and Water*. Herald Press.

Miller, Ivan J., and Della Miller. *History of the Conservative Mennonite Conference, 1910-1985*.

Nolt, Steven M. *A History of the Amish*. Good Books.

Redekop, Calvin. *Mennonite Society*. Johns Hopkins University Press.

Scott, Stephen. *An Introduction to Old Order and Conservative Mennonite Groups*. Good Books.

Wittlinger, Carlton O. *Quest For Piety and Obedience*. Evangel Press.

Index of Churches

Christian Nelson Hostetter is a graduate of Messiah Academy and Junior College at Grantham, Pennsylvania. He holds a BA in Sociology from Goshen College, Indiana, and is a graduate of Pittsburgh Institute of Mortuary Science. He has done additional studies at Government Staff College, Battle Creek, Michigan, now Emergency Management Institute at Emmitsburg, Maryland, and at the Institute of Behavioral Science, University of Colorado at Boulder and the Institute of Emergency Preparedness at University of Southern California at Los Angeles.

During World War II he served over four years in Civilian Public Service at Grottoes, Virginia; Mulberry, Florida; Ypsilanti, Michigan; and Cayey and LaPlata, Puerto Rico.

Nelson married the former Esther Miller from Ohio and they have a daughter, son, and a grandson. In their early career years they owned and operated a convalescent and emergency ambulance service in West Liberty, Ohio, funeral homes in West Liberty and Zanesfield, and monument companies in Urbana and West Liberty. While in Ohio he served part-time as Emergency Services Manager for Logan County and as coordinator for Western Ohio Mennonite Disaster Service Unit.

In later career years Nelson served as executive coordinator for Mennonite Disaster Service, responsible for the States, Canada, and the Caribbean. In recent years he served as a volunteer consultant for Church World Service National Disaster Response, and a staff person in Church Disaster Relief for Pennsylvania Catholic Conference, Pennsylvania Council of Churches, Kentucky Council of Churches, and West Virginia Council of Churches.

The Hostetters make their seasonal homes in Akron, Pennsylvania, and Sarasota, Florida. They are members of the Akron Mennonite Church and associate members of the Bahia Vista Mennonite Church in Sarasota.